# THE HEALTHCARE SUPPLY CHAIN

Best Practices for Operating at the Intersection of
Cost, Quality, and Outcomes

## SECOND EDITION

*Consulting Editor*
Christopher J. O'Connor

*Foreword by*
Lee H. Perlman

ISBN: 978-0-692-95744-8

Cover and book design by Dieter Klipstein.

Printed in the United States of America.

For information on bulk purchases, please contact gnyhapress@gnyha.org.

# Contents

# Foreword

As a longtime healthcare executive, I never take for granted the important role our industry plays in people's lives. From the manufacturing plant worker to the supply chain manager to the nurse at a patient's bedside, we all strive to improve patient care and the healthcare delivery system.

As you read this, the healthcare delivery system is experiencing a seismic shift. There are new technologies and advanced data, new government regulations, and the accompanying transition from fee-for-service reimbursement to value-based, patient-centered care. The landscape seems to change daily. Those changes are both tangible and challenging for the healthcare supply chain, and require continuous improvement and the nimbleness to evolve as the industry evolves.

The first edition of this book, *Healthcare Supply Chain at the Intersection of Cost, Quality, and Outcomes,* presented the cost, quality, and outcomes (CQO) framework and served as a resource guide for the Hospital Supply Chain Performance Self-Assessment™, a tool created by Nexera's team of subject matter experts. This tool enables hospital and health system leaders to benchmark current supply chain performance against 12 focus areas and outlines steps to help healthcare organizations move toward a strategic supply chain that operates at the intersection of CQO.

In the spirit of continuous improvement, we have written a second edition of this book. This edition outlines best practices and key performance indicators. It also includes new standards that supply chain professionals are being held to (such as an increased focus on quality) so that they can more accurately benchmark their performance based on today's evolving clinical and economic environment.

Supplies—whether they be as simple as gauze or as complex as neurostimulators—are the crux of patient care. I have long said that while healthcare requires a complicated set of systems and processes, ultimately only two things are needed to care for patients: staff and "stuff." While the supply chain is involved in nearly every supply transaction a hospital makes, in the past it wasn't considered a strategic component of hospital operations.

That was yesterday. Today's healthcare leaders increasingly understand that hospital supply chain experts play a major role in value-based, patient-centered care. Hospital supplies must not only be evaluated based on price, they must be evaluated based on how a particular product may impact an episode of care. Leaders must look at current processes and care pathways to examine all the variables that can contribute to case delays or less than optimal care. Simply put, the supply chain plays an important role in value-based decision-making.

CQO gives supply chain professionals a framework to achieve their strategic objective. We know the supply chain reduces costs. Now it must become more clinically integrated and help improve patient outcomes.

This book, which centers on best practices, provides guidance for how supply chain professionals can succeed in this new environment. The more we understand and embrace our part in value-based, patient-centered care, the more we will help create a better healthcare delivery system. And that, after all, is why we do what we do.

Enjoy the book.

**Lee H. Perlman** | President, GNYHA Ventures
Chief Financial Officer and Executive Vice President,
Greater New York Hospital Association

*Lee Perlman is the President of GNYHA Ventures, the for-profit business arm of the Greater New York Hospital Association. One of the industry's most passionate leaders about the marriage of business and science in healthcare management and procurement, Mr. Perlman is a steadfast advocate for price transparency, comparative effectiveness in the supply chain, and lowering healthcare providers' cost of doing business while maintaining greater resources for direct patient care.*

# Acknowledgments

*The Healthcare Supply Chain: Best Practices for Operating at the Intersection of Cost, Quality, and Outcomes* is the product of intense collaboration between supply chain experts from Acurity, Inc. (a healthcare group purchasing organization and supply chain resource) and Nexera, Inc. (a healthcare consulting firm). Acurity and Nexera are subsidiaries of GNYHA Ventures, Inc., the business arm of the Greater New York Hospital Association (GNYHA).

The Cost, Quality, and Outcomes Movement has made substantial progress since the release of our 2015 book, *Healthcare Supply Chain at the Intersection of Cost, Quality, and Outcomes*, which identified the relationship between the healthcare supply chain and CQO. We must now consider what will be required of the supply chain going forward and offer the industry further guidance about how to embrace new challenges and deliver meaningful value in a rapidly evolving healthcare landscape.

In late 2016, a Steering Committee of Acurity and Nexera executives gathered to provide direction for our second edition. As a result of those discussions, this book takes a deeper look at how supply chain professionals can achieve top-line performance in every area of supply chain operations. To formulate the core content, Project Content Committees were created based on individuals' areas of expertise. They spent countless hours brainstorming, outlining, writing, reviewing, and refining every chapter and every best practice to ensure that this book would be useful for healthcare leaders, supply chain professionals in different stages of their careers, healthcare vendors, and students. The names of these individuals are listed as contributors in each chapter. I am confident that everyone who reads this book will take away examples of how they can contribute to the evolution and improvement of the healthcare supply chain.

I would like to thank GNYHA President Kenneth E. Raske, GNYHA Ventures President Lee H. Perlman, the GNYHA Board of Governors, and the GNYHA Ventures Board of Directors for continuing to create an environment that welcomes, encourages, and nurtures new ideas. Their unwavering commitment, forward thinking, and willingness to invest resources in projects that have the potential to bring significant value to our customers and industry make the pursuit of efforts like these possible.

I would also like to express my sincere thanks and appreciation to the individuals below who helped develop this book. Without their expertise and both individual and collective contributions, this project would not have come to fruition.

- Jeffrey Ashkenase, Executive Vice President, Acurity and Nexera
- Michael Berger, Manager, Nexera
- Kristin A. Boehm, MD, Physician Advisor, Nexera
- Michelle Byalick, Vice President, GNYHA Ventures
- Joseph S. Cirillo, Senior Director, Acurity
- Emily Coakley, Editor at Large, GNYHA
- Brian Conway, Senior Vice President, GNYHA and GNYHA Ventures
- Amy E. Cretella, Director, Acurity and Nexera
- Cathy Cudmore, Assistant Vice President, Acurity
- Lyn Cusanello, Director, Nexera
- Lisa Fishelberg, Associate Vice President, Acurity
- Jay Fligstein, Senior Vice President, Acurity
- Francine Freise, Director, Acurity
- Alison Flynn Gaffney, Senior Vice President, Acurity and Nexera*
- Ritika Ghose, Senior Consultant, Nexera
- Tim Glennon, RN, Vice President, Nexera
- Martin Glick, Vice President, Acurity
- Barbara A. Green, PhD, Senior Vice President, GNYHA Ventures
- Adam Gross, Contract Manager, Acurity

- Kenneth Hecht, Director, Acurity
- Michelle Jacobs, Assistant Vice President, GNYHA Ventures
- Mia James, RN, Director, Nexera
- Michael L. Jones, Director, Nexera
- Robert J. Karcher, Senior Vice President, Acurity
- Dieter Klipstein, Creative Director, GNYHA Ventures
- Edward Lieber, Editor, GNYHA
- Thomas McLoughlin, Assistant Vice President, Acurity
- Sandra A. Monacelli, RN, Vice President, Nexera
- Michael Petretta, Director, Acurity
- Robert Rizzi, Consultant, Nexera
- Kenneth Scher, Senior Manager, Nexera
- Alexandra Schonholz, Senior Communications Manager, GNYHA Ventures
- Steven Schramm, Director, Acurity
- Praful Shah, Vice President, Acurity
- Perry Sham, Senior Vice President, Nexera
- Dean G. Sheffield, Assistant Vice President, Nexera
- Kristin Stephens, Senior Director, GNYHA
- Ann Vayos, Vice President, Acurity
- Bruce C. Vladeck, PhD, Senior Advisor, Nexera*
- Glenn Wexler, Vice President and Associate General Counsel, GNYHA Ventures

*denotes former employee at time of publication

In addition, I would like to thank the hospitals and health systems that agreed to let their stories be told in this book so that others can learn from their experience: Hartford HealthCare, NYC Health + Hospitals, Kaleida Health, Hospital for Special Surgery, St. Luke's Cornwall Hospital, Mount Sinai Health System, and The University of Tennessee Medical Center.

Finally, I want to thank my colleagues at the Association for Healthcare Resource & Materials Management (AHRMM) and the supply chain executives who are AHRMM members for their continuing support of CQO. Their enthusiastic embrace of this concept has transformed CQO from a local idea to a national movement, one that is leading to a fundamental paradigm shift in understanding the role that the supply chain plays and its important position in hospital and health system management.

On behalf of everyone who has been involved in this project, I am pleased to share *The Healthcare Supply Chain: Best Practices for Operating at the Intersection of Cost, Quality, and Outcomes*. This edition is intended as a best practice guide that details how the supply chain can make incremental improvements in each area of operations and build upon transactional successes to achieve more strategic objectives that focus on improving care quality and reducing total operating expenses. From there, hospital and health system readers can measure their own performance through the Hospital Supply Chain Performance Self-Assessment and look back at specific chapters for guidance about the areas in which they require the most improvement.

I encourage readers who have questions or who want to expand upon the information provided in any chapter of this book to contact our experts at Acurity and Nexera. This book is intended to be a valuable, motivational resource for healthcare organizations in their pursuit of CQO. Our understanding of supply chain management and its impact on CQO will continue to evolve and mature, and we are happy to continue to share this knowledge with you.

**Christopher J. O'Connor**
January 2018

# Introduction

For some time now, America's healthcare delivery system has been in a state of intense political flux. However, despite a backdrop of profound disagreement and uncertainty, one healthcare trend has remained constant: the gradual but consistent movement away from the fee-for-service reimbursement model.

For hospitals, that has meant a transition to reimbursement models that reward the quality of care over the number of visits and tests ordered. This shift to value-based, patient-centered care is certainly a move in the right direction—providers are being paid to do the right thing and penalized if they don't—but it is also a significant challenge for healthcare professionals long accustomed to fee-for-service methods and unaccustomed to the vast data and cultural changes that are necessary to be successful (and financially viable) in this new environment.

Today, providers must be able to quantify and weigh the impact of total healthcare delivery costs against patient and financial outcomes. Hospitals must evaluate the clinical effectiveness of a device compared to its functional equivalent by examining the outcomes of the procedures in which each have been used. Providers might see a greater financial return by using a device that is more expensive at the outset if there is evidence that it is connected to better patient outcomes. The decision to use the costlier but more clinically effective device could, in fact, result in fewer readmissions or infections. Providers are also less likely to be hit with related payment penalties and have a greater chance of being fully reimbursed by payers (Medicare, Medicaid, other third-party payers) for those episodes of care.

This value-based reimbursement system rewards providers who decrease costs while improving quality and outcomes, creating a better, more cost-effective healthcare system. This is called operating at the intersection of cost, quality, and outcomes—also known as CQO. Most healthcare professionals want to achieve this goal, but they may not truly understand *how* to achieve it given their institution's culture, data, and resources. In addition, the playing field has changed. Some physicians may be perceived as performing too many procedures and must learn to operate under new standards of care. Service line leaders who have become accustomed to ordering the latest technology with little or no oversight must accept new mandates that require an evidence-based motivation that is driven by how that new technology will improve patient outcomes. Healthcare leaders can use CQO to offer their workforce a framework for initiating the multidisciplinary collaboration and organization-wide acceptance that is needed to meet their value-based goals.

## The Origins of Health Insurance in the United States

### AN EMPLOYER-BASED, COST-BASED SYSTEM

Between the late 1920s and the early 1970s, the basic structure of the U.S. healthcare insurance system was formed, including the earliest forms of private health coverage around 1929, the rise of employer-based health insurance in the 1940s, and the enactment of the Medicare and Medicaid programs in 1965, which provided healthcare coverage to elderly and low-income Americans. During this time, hospital services were paid for by both private and public insurance programs on the basis of a retrospective, cost-based reimbursement system under which they were reimbursed for their actual cost of goods and services plus an overhead amount.[1,2] There were no incentives for hospitals or other providers to manage costs, so from a supply chain perspective the price of products was of little significance. Supply chain management was primarily concerned with transactional metrics, such as fill rates, the accuracy of product orders, and the timeliness of shipments.[3]

## THE ERA OF COST CONTAINMENT

The virtually open-ended reimbursement system—coupled with major advancements in medical technology—resulted in rapidly escalating healthcare costs. Between 1967 and 1983, for example, Medicare's annual hospital disbursements rose from $3 billion to $37 billion.[2] This sparked concern among policymakers, who began taking steps to curb growth in health spending. Their efforts embraced such payment and care delivery models as capitation and managed care, leading to the eventual adoption by Medicare of the prospective payment system, which pays hospitals flat rates based on diagnosis-related groups (DRGs). Hospital purchases and procurement practices became a major focal point for hospital and health system executives, which resulted in purchasing decisions that were driven largely by cost.

## LINKING COST WITH QUALITY AND OUTCOMES

Cost containment remained a concern among health policymakers for roughly two decades. At the turn of the 21st century, however, attention began to shift to quality and outcomes in response to studies pointing to wide variations in quality and outcomes by procedure, provider, and geography that were difficult to explain. This led to such initiatives as value-based purchasing and pay-for-performance. While these initiatives had varying degrees of success, they triggered a major structural shift in the healthcare delivery system from one that was heavily reliant on hospitals and inpatient services to one that emphasized fewer hospitals, shorter hospital stays, and more outpatient and community-based care.

Enter the Affordable Care Act (ACA), President Barack Obama's comprehensive health reform initiative, which was enacted in 2010. This sweeping health reform law had two primary goals: making health insurance coverage available to virtually all uninsured or underinsured Americans, and improving the efficiency and quality of the healthcare delivery system.

The ACA remains a topic of deep political debate, and efforts to repeal and replace it will continue in 2018 and possibly beyond.

The history of healthcare delivery reveals how the function of the supply chain has evolved alongside reimbursement policies—from unfettered purchasing when reimbursement was largely open-ended to a focus on cost containment as healthcare spending escalated. This era is no different. In fact, the supply chain has never been more important or in a better position to make a positive impact on healthcare and patients' lives.

Supply chain executives sit at the center of purchasing decisions and work across disciplines. They affect—though sometimes indirectly—nearly every step of patient care delivery. This makes them particularly well suited to lead CQO initiatives. But while CQO provides the decision-making framework, hospital leaders must still find ways to ingrain these practices across their organizations. This is no easy task, but it's easier when you know where to start. The first step lies in readying the supply chain for value-based care so that it can serve as the champion of CQO. This can be viewed as a succession of smaller steps:

## Transactional

The initial step is transactional. A transactional supply chain is focused on price improvement and performing fundamental supply chain practices.

## Engage a Network

The next step for supply chain is engaging a network of product end users (e.g., physicians, clinicians, and service line leaders) and vendors. Supply chain professionals must understand the needs of others and incorporate feedback into the sourcing process to make the most effective evidence-based purchasing decisions. This greater level of understanding helps move the provider-supplier conversation from one of price over value to one of healthcare issues over supply chain issues. It also cultivates a relationship that is more truly aligned with value-based care.

## Transform the Culture

When the supply chain has the support of an expanded network and executive leadership, department leaders are better positioned to make the necessary cultural and structural adjustments to facilitate change and begin examining and familiarizing their teams with alternative data sets (e.g., outcomes, variability, physician use) so that they are armed to make better-informed, value-based purchasing decisions.

## Create an Integrated Model

An integrated model is achieved when purchasing goals are aligned organization-wide. Hospital administration, end users, and supply chain are employing data to focus on how products are used and the differences in quality based upon the total cost of an episode of care.

## Cost, Quality, and Outcomes

When all stakeholders are focused on securing results that decrease costs while improving quality and outcomes, the organization and its supply chain are operating at the intersection of CQO.

FIGURE 1

# Getting Supply Chain to CQO

## Create an Integrated Model

CHARACTERISTICS

- Widely accepted, standardized supply chain practices
- Physician-led value analysis in place
- Standardized supply chain analytics, metrics, and dashboards are used to make informed, value-based decisions
- Use of analytics drives outcomes-based contracts and initiatives

## Transform the Culture

CHARACTERISTICS

- Shifting supply chain governance to be more involved in critical decision-making
- Developing use of alternative data sets
- Putting value analysis in place
- Greater focus on process improvement
- Working on staff development and education

## Engage a Network

CHARACTERISTICS

- Cultivating internal and external relationships
- Securing clinical and service line champions for most specialities
- Beginning to incorporate feedback into the sourcing process

## Transactional

CHARACTERISTICS

- Focus on day-to-day supply chain operations
- Using basic supply chain technology and data sets
- Working on supply chain automation

Source: Acurity, Inc. and Nexera, Inc.

Physician engagement and data are integral to this progression. It is also vital to have a supply chain that is working at optimal performance in all of its functional areas. While supply chain leaders can begin to build relationships with end users and administrators, those connections will continue to be challenged if supply chain representatives aren't able to secure meaningful data to back up purchasing decisions, ensure that necessary items are kept in inventory, and make certain that current practices aren't leading to product waste or excess costs (since supply chain-related expenses can represent the majority of an organization's total budget). In this way, all areas of supply chain operations have a direct link to both downstream clinical and financial initiatives and a hospital's ability to operate at the intersection of CQO.

FIGURE 2
## Supply Chain Operations

Source: Nexera, Inc.

*This diagram illustrates the different areas of supply chain operations in order to demonstrate that it is a holistic process and, therefore, performance in one area links directly to performance in the next.*

The Supply Chain Operations diagram (see Figure 2) outlines every area that impacts the overall performance of a hospital or health system's supply chain. This book has been developed using these elements in an order that reflects the steps necessary to get to CQO. The first section—Getting Started—reviews the areas that are the backbone of the change management required to operate at the intersection of CQO. The book's best practices cannot be fully accomplished and sustained without addressing the areas outlined in the first chapter. The second section—Building the Foundation—includes best practices for achieving optimal performance in supply chain's functional areas. These chapters have been written to apply to an array of providers. No matter where a hospital's supply chain is on the path to CQO, this book will provide guidance for how it can make incremental improvements and work toward optimal performance. The next section—Operating at the Intersection of Cost, Quality, and Outcomes—includes chapters focused on the areas that are most closely tied to supply chain operations in a value-based environment. For example, value analysis, when performed properly, is a method for enabling CQO-based initiatives. The value analysis chapter outlines best practices for implementing a physician-led process in your organization. Finally, our contracting-focused chapter addresses how the supply chain can utilize the data and structure achieved by implementing all of the best practices to enter into strategic, value-based purchasing arrangements, such as vendor contracts based on product performance as they relate to patient outcomes.

The healthcare supply chain must evolve in line with the industry's shift to value-based reimbursement, as the performance and effectiveness of the supply chain are integral to a provider's ability to deliver quality, cost-effective care in a challenging economy. The ability to take a more strategic approach to product selection, looking for the best value (examining total cost, quality, and outcomes) rather than simply the lowest price, begins with the supply chain. Ensuring the successful and sustainable advancement of this level of decision-making across a healthcare organization requires that all functional areas of the supply chain operate at peak performance.

This book is designed to serve as a guide to enhancing the strategic contributions of the healthcare supply chain in a way that is most meaningful to hospitals' and health systems' value-based goals.

Let's get started.

1. T.C. Buchmueller and Monheit, A.C., "Employer-Sponsored Health Insurance and the Promise of Health Insurance Reform," *National Bureau of Economic Review*, (April 2009). http://www.nber.org/papers/w14839 (accessed October 25, 2017).
2. P. Gottlober, Brady, T., Robinson, B., Davis, T., "Medicare Hospital Prospective Payment System: How DRG Rates are Calculated and Updated." *Office of the Inspector General, Office of Evaluations, Region IX*, (August 2001). https://oig.hhs.gov/oei/reports/oei-09-00-00200.pdf (accessed October 25, 2017).
3. M. Darling and Wise, S., "Not your father's supply chain: Following best practices to manage inventory can help you save big," *Materials Management in Health Care* vol. 19, no. 4 (April 2010); 30-33.

# Getting Started

I.

# The Fundamentals:
# What needs to be established in
# the pursuit of best practice

CONTRIBUTORS

Lisa Fishelberg | Jay Fligstein | Alison Flynn Gaffney | Kenneth Scher | Perry Sham

Applying value-based principles across an entire organization requires change management. People, process, and culture are the backbone of any change management. The key to success for hospital leaders is to find ways to operationalize these essential elements. To establish a solid foundation for operating at the intersection of cost, quality, and outcomes (CQO), hospital leaders should make the following best practices a regular feature of their operations. These best practices will help put organizations in a position not only to make strategic improvements, but to sustain their progress by setting internal controls, adopting a culture of continuous process improvement, and keeping staff properly educated.

BEST PRACTICE
**Establish internal controls for the supply chain**
Some internal controls are fundamental. But by ensuring a standard, ethical way of working, operations can be streamlined and risk (negative outcomes) mitigated. High-performing institutions make a concerted effort to ensure that the practice of setting internal controls for clinical areas is also applied to the business side of their organizations, including the supply chain. Therefore,

internal controls that have set standards, policies, and procedures should be created for all areas of supply chain operations (data management/analytics, requisitioning, purchasing, receiving, distribution, inventory management, value analysis, and contracting).

There are two main components of internal controls: 1) putting policies in place that spell out staff responsibilities, establish protocols, and reduce errors and 2) ensuring that those policies are followed. Effective internal controls take people and process into consideration first and the use of technology second. Staff should receive training on their part in the process, learn what checks and balances are in place, and know their organization's policy for maintaining ethical business practices (e.g., to avoid fraud and abuse, the person who creates a purchase order [PO] shouldn't be the person who processes the payment). Technology can then be employed to make processes more efficient and to track organization-wide adherence.

Technology should not be considered the way to end a problem but rather a tool to enhance performance by automating management controls and establishing more consistent workflows. For example, everyone should be taught how to use a standardized (organization-wide) requisition system. Then an electronic approval process can be employed to keep a record of sign-offs and track where steps were skipped or where the process can be improved. Internal controls are also closely tied to risk management. Effective internal controls help identify risk, such as product expirations, and aid in the safe introduction of new products. Technology can enhance these controls by preventing situations that might otherwise occur through human error.

Internal control reviews should be conducted regularly and when there have been recent changes to management systems or operations. These reviews can determine if the controls are serving their intended purpose (sustaining progress and performance) or if there are areas for improvement. Management should also consider the return on investment (ROI) for approval pathways related to specific policies. While it is important to enforce approval processes for certain activities—especially those that result in a cost to the organization—the time devoted to this effort must also be factored in. As a general rule of thumb, develop the shortest approval path possible while still ensuring procedural compliance. First, however, organizations should have good budget controls in place.

BEST PRACTICE
## Promote continuous process improvement
Smart organizations are constantly looking for ways to improve. Formalizing continuous process improvement offers a number of benefits. First, it is an organizational commitment to excellence. Second, it helps reduce waste. It can also increase operating efficiency by isolating problems that obstruct workflow. As a result, process improvement solutions can be formulated and implemented, then their impact can be evaluated. This, in turn, can have a positive effect on employee and patient satisfaction.

Because every day brings a new challenge, the best supply chain professionals are problem solvers. Setting internal controls and adopting a culture of continuous process improvement can lead to fewer issues and more proactive responses, allowing the supply chain time to focus on strategy. However, there are certain prerequisites.

1. **Leadership Support:** Any change in operational approach must begin at the top. Management—both organization-wide and department-specific—should focus on identifying problems and developing internal controls to avoid repeating them. The process should be clearly communicated and reinforced with the message that it is everyone's responsibility to make sure that it is followed. And *everyone* should follow the established process—from the top down. The example set by leadership is generally reflected in the level of staff acceptance.

2. **Metrics:** Information is vital to changing behavior because evidence inspires action. Using metrics can help the supply chain catch issues before they turn into problems. Ask leading questions related to departmental responsibilities (such as how much of a certain product is the hospital buying), then optimize the use of technology to pinpoint where there are opportunities for improvement. Data reviews and reports should be common practice.

3. **Collaboration:** The participation of internal and external stakeholders is vital to the success of continuous process improvement. Team members should be empowered to ask questions, identify issues, and provide suggestions. People are more likely to comply with processes if they feel that they are part of the solution. In time, internal controls and continuous process

improvement should become everyday practice. External stakeholders, such as group purchasing organizations (GPOs), vendors, and professional associations can be good sources of information about how others have dealt with similar issues.

4. **Evaluation:** Just as an organization should evaluate the effectiveness of its internal controls, it should also regularly assess its dedication to continuous process improvement. This includes asking if everything possible is being done to move processes to best practice as well as establishing key performance indicators. Remember, there is always room for improvement.

BEST PRACTICE
## Provide staff education

To transform the supply chain from transactional to strategic, education is crucial. Investing in staff education helps employees feel more connected to and invested in their work, which has a direct impact on productivity. For purposes of this book, education encompasses the following:

1. **Job-Based Training:** Members of the supply chain team should be trained in their departmental role to create efficiency as well as adherence to protocols. Adopting a culture of continuous process improvement helps ensure that the organization is tracking the success of its supply chain procedures based on overall supply chain performance. The results of these efforts will dictate if more or better training is necessary.

    It is also best practice to cross-train staff in different areas of the supply chain to make certain that operations continue to run smoothly when someone goes on vacation, takes an extended leave, or resigns.

2. **Broadening the Supply Chain Skill Set:** The role of the supply chain professional has undergone tremendous change. The responsibilities of supply chain executives have traditionally focused on negotiating, ordering, receiving, and distributing medical supplies. Today, these professionals are responsible for total supply management, sometimes referred to as the value chain (to reflect the increased focus on quality). The demand to have supply chain professionals become strategic contributors to a provider's value-based goals requires them to broaden their understanding of what those objectives are as well as to understand the clinical and financial aspects

of their profession, including reimbursement policies, incentives, and penalties; evidence-based medicine; and population health management.

Hospital and department leaders should support the value-based education of their supply chain team by creating educational programs that use internal resources by enlisting the help of a strategic partner—such as a GPO or contracted vendor—or by using other readily available resources—such as conferences, webinars, and podcasts—from such professional associations as the Association for Healthcare Resource & Materials Management, Institute for Supply Management, American College of Healthcare Executives, etc. Encourage supply chain employees to receive and maintain certificates specific to their field, such as a Certified Materials & Resource Professional (CMRP).

Hospital administrators must understand the current role of the supply chain profession and offer those individuals—especially seasoned professionals—the means to evolve.

3. **Provide Cross-Disciplinary Education:** Supply chain professionals are hard pressed to make value-based decisions if they don't have the support of clinicians. Hospital leaders should help break down internal silos and create collaborative forums in which supply chain leaders can build relationships with physicians, nurses, and other clinicians to better understand their needs. Similarly, information about clinical and physician preference products should be included in educational programs that are created for supply chain staff. That way the supply chain team can better understand the needs of their clinical counterparts and contribute to value analysis discussions in a more meaningful way. They can also better represent the organization's needs during sourcing negotiations.

It is also important to teach clinicians about supply chain operations. Clinicians—and to a certain extent hospital administrators—need an in-depth understanding of how the supply chain's individual components operate in order to truly appreciate the positive results associated with a supply chain that runs smoothly versus the potential disruptions and expensive consequences associated with the breakdown of any individual supply chain component. Clinicians, in particular, must understand their role in the supply chain process and its potential to affect outcomes.

A regularly scheduled, formalized, cross-disciplinary educational program is critical to achieving value-based goals.

4. **Support for Current and Future Generations:** There are several generations in the workforce. Hospitals must consider how they can attract new talent into the healthcare supply chain. Today's supply chain professionals have a variety of backgrounds. Some have degrees and years of on-the-job hospital experience while others have risen through the ranks by dint of hard work or circumstance.

Teaching employees about how different generations can work together helps increase productivity. A workplace culture that supports the ongoing development of a more strategic supply chain skill set helps level the playing field for seasoned professionals while also helping to attract young, capable professionals by encouraging them to pursue a career in the industry.

During the recruitment process, consider the skill sets that are likely to be required of future supply chain professionals, such as the ability to work with predictive analytics. This will help attract younger generations and ensure that the department is hiring the right people.

# Supply Chain Education in Action

*An example of how education can improve productivity
and support supply chain transformation*

FUNDAMENTAL PRACTICE
**Supply chain education program**

PROVIDER
**Academic medical center**

## Background

To help meet the medical center's goal of providing the best possible care, the supply chain department recognized the need to improve its value through staff development. The training was meant to help supply chain staff have more productive conversations with clinical stakeholders. It was also intended to give them a better, more holistic understanding of the supply chain's role and its potential impact on the hospital, physicians, and patients.

The program included instruction about the Affordable Care Act, the Institute for Healthcare Improvement (IHI) Triple Aim, health reform, and how each impacted the hospital. Additionally, leadership wanted to improve the job satisfaction of the team through a better understanding of the industry and its unique challenges, and how each team member plays a vital role in addressing those challenges.

Four objectives were identified on a department-specific and organization-wide basis:

- Look at all criteria in product selection, not just cost
- Be aware that cost savings now may result in a penalty later
- Have a robust, interdisciplinary value analysis program
- Begin to consider value-based contracts with suppliers

**Methodology**

A supply chain education program was established with support from the health system's GPO in which all supply chain team members (buyers, sourcing and contracting, and data analytics) receive ongoing education. The first 90-minute session included the following:

- Understanding the components of the Triple Aim (a framework developed by the IHI that describes an approach to optimizing health system performance)
- Understanding the impact of the three Centers for Medicare & Medicaid Services (CMS) performance-based programs (value-based purchasing, hospital-acquired conditions, and readmission reduction) on hospitals and in supply chain
- Understanding the impact that the new physician performance measures will have on hospitals and supply chain

To gain a better comprehension of the industry, the sessions included a discussion of what other hospital supply chains were currently doing to tackle value-based care. Participants were given metrics specific to the hospital to guide a conversation about where they stand today and where they need to go with regard to the CMS performance-based programs. Discussions about the organization's pipeline were also incorporated, which tied in contracting strategies, value analysis, and team discussions as they relate to CQO principles.

The program also included information about how value-based care impacts revenue growth, penalties incurred, and physician recruitment and retention. The sessions emphasized the need to be adaptable in the ever-changing healthcare landscape.

## Results

Since implementing the program, staff has expressed both satisfaction and gratitude. Specifically, there is a shared appreciation of leadership's willingness to invest in the team's professional growth, which has allowed them to improve themselves, to learn things related to healthcare that extend beyond their day-to-day responsibilities, and to expand their awareness of their part in the bigger picture.

The medical center's GPO has been engaged to support ongoing education on a quarterly basis.

# Building the
# Foundation

work for the best practices in every chapter of this book. Clean data enables more efficient procurement because it reduces confusion and unnecessary back-and-forth communication between the staff requesting an item and the supply chain staff. Carefully managing this data facilitates all analysis efforts, from tracking organizational processes to more strategic deep dives into product and protocol efficacy and financial outcomes. Obtaining precise data, however, requires an effective technology infrastructure to support it.

While providers have traditionally used different systems for human resources, accounting, and materials management, hospitals and health systems have increasingly moved to enterprise resource planning (ERP) systems, a technology that integrates these disparate programs under one umbrella to streamline processes and better support cost management. However, while ERPs are best practice, they aren't the only solution. A well-maintained standalone materials management information system (MMIS) should be able to provide the relevant data to support cost management initiatives. Having all of a health system's key functions under one platform promotes efficiency and other benefits, but the goal is to be able to extract and analyze accurate data to drive decision-making and monitoring. When used properly, MMIS data can play an enormous role in helping hospital leaders determine the cost per case. When an MMIS is linked to clinical and financial data, a report documenting a supply's impact on a patient outcome (e.g., average length of stay and readmission rate) can be analyzed down to the physician level to help hospitals make more educated purchasing decisions.

There's a strong case to be made for investing in supply chain infrastructure. When trying to convince decision-makers, supply chain leaders should first research the benefit to the hospital's bottom line. Technology is a strategic asset that can help the supply chain department manage expenses effectively. Such an investment, however, must be about more than technology. A corresponding investment in human capital is essential.

BEST PRACTICE
## Create and maintain a clean, robust item master
In the supply chain, the first area of data management focus should be the hospital's item master, which is ideally a single repository of nearly every product a hospital buys and uses. Essentially, it is the supply chain's source of truth. The data stored in the item master is the foundation for everything involved in supply chain management. From placing and managing orders

to compiling reports and analytics to pricing, contracting, inventory, and controlling spend, the accuracy of the data within the item master determines the effectiveness of the supply chain.

*Create a process for entering additions to the item master*
The way in which the item master is amended is vitally important for controlling expenses. Limit the number of staff members who have the authority to modify the item master, and ensure that those who have authority are continuously trained and cognizant of the organization's nomenclature for product fields. Create an approval hierarchy for all item master changes. This policy should be communicated to medical staff and C-suite executives to make certain that all requests for supplies go through purchasing.

Include key data fields for each entry in the item master. This will help identify the item so that the correct one is ordered.

---

**Primary Fields**
- Item master number
- Vendor part number
- Vendor name
- Vendor ID
- Manufacturer part number
- Manufacturer name
- Manufacturer ID
- Item description
- Item price
- Unit of measure (UOM)
- UOM conversion factor (quantity of each)

**To further enhance reporting, additional recommended fields include**
- HCPCS (Health Care Procedure Coding System) number
- GTIN (Global Trade Item Number)
- UNSPSC® (United Nations Standard Products and Services Code)
- CDM code (chargemaster code)
- Expense code

---

If latex-free gloves need to be ordered, for example, consider the nomenclature under which they are listed in the item master ("glove, latex-free," "latex-free glove," both, neither). Without a clear process for entering item master information, hospitals run the risk of accumulating duplicates or obsolete products, entering inaccurate information, and creating muddled hospital records of department-wide or organization-wide use and spend.

An example of standard nomenclature is as follows:

| NOUN | ADJECTIVE | VERB | SIZE | SHAPE* | COLOR |
|------|-----------|------|------|--------|-------|
| GLOVE | NITRILE | EXAM | LARGE | | BLUE |

*if applicable

Using this nomenclature, when someone searches for "glove," a more comprehensive list of items will appear.

Some supply chain professionals advocate loading every contracted product into the item master, regardless of whether the product is actually being used by the facility or not. However, one contract can contain hundreds—even thousands—of individual products. Correctly adding each of those products (and all of their required data points) to the item master can require enormous resources and be a significant administrative burden to maintain. Facilities should weigh the utility gained from loading a complete product catalog into their item master (on the assumption that they may order a product sometime in the future) versus loading only the products that are used most often.

*Limit the use of non-catalog items and special requests*

A hospital's data is composed of two primary data sets: the item master (items approved for purchase and assigned an MMIS number) and PO history (all items that a hospital has ordered, regardless of whether they are in the item master). Within the item master, items can further be classified as stock (held in inventory) or non-stock (items that are ordered periodically but not frequently enough to be held in inventory). Purchases that are not included in the item master are typically one-time purchases and called non-catalog items or special orders/requests. Examples include purchased services, capital equipment, maintenance, and some physician preference items. As these items are not in the item master, this often creates an inability to aggregate the data necessary to gain maximum benefit from supply chain analytics. When looking at cost-saving opportunities, these items can skew or impact a hospital's decisions, as the information needed is not always available to prepare accurate analyses. Supply chain departments must rely on manual data manipulation in order to compile the item master data with the non-catalog items in order to fully understand their purchasing power and physician use patterns. It is best practice to limit non-catalog items and special requests.

*Always check item master information before entering*

Though time-consuming at the front end, checking the information that is entered into the item master helps to ensure that you are working with accurate data. Ask vendors and manufacturers to send a current item file based on their hospital's use that includes full item detail (such as UOM, pricing, etc.). Keep in mind, however, that neither vendors nor manufacturers always provide the right information. Similarly, a contract may list a product using a series of numbers separated by dashes. But when the same item number is entered into the vendor's electronic data interchange (EDI) system, the dashes are not recognized and the order is rejected. Validating this information as part of the entry process can prevent delays down the line. Ideally, this process is automated.

*Create a process for maintaining a normalized (clean) item master*
Supply chain should assign someone (or several people) with extensive product knowledge to review and update the item master on a regular basis using the defined entry procedures. This individual can also review the item master against the hospital's PO history to remove items that are not used by the hospital for a specific, agreed upon time frame (e.g., 24 months) to keep it organized and up-to-date. These responsibilities can also be outsourced. After making any mass update, run an item master extract to confirm that changes have been completed correctly.

To maintain a useful, accurate item master, supply chain staff must also create a process for monitoring contract expirations. An established procedure helps ensure that the contract for a heavily used item is renewed ahead of time. Conversely, it can help catch an order being placed for an item whose contract has recently expired.

BEST PRACTICE
## Standardize data using unique identifiers
The supply chain should consider methods for standardizing data collected from different sources. It is best practice to use the American National Standards Institute's (ANSI) system for UOMs (e.g., CA instead of CS for case).

One complication that hospitals face is the lack of an industry-wide standard for product numbers. Distributors use vendor part numbers, and manufacturers use their own numbers. Consequently, hospitals must maintain both numbers in the item master, as it's sometimes necessary to order from both the manufacturer and the distributor.

Besides manufacturer and distributor product numbers, there are other unique identifiers that can help analyze data. The HCPCS, GTIN, UNSPSC as well as the UDI (Unique Device Identification) and GLN (Global Location Number) can be used to help internal data reconciliation decisions, such as charge coding, expense coding, and ship-to or deliver-to creation.

## Content Management Services

Hospitals can purchase third-party content management services that cleanse item masters by identifying such data gaps as incorrect packaging information, outdated vendor information (vendors or product lines are frequently acquired by other vendors), or different product descriptions. These services also provide data fields that may be difficult for a hospital to acquire on its own (e.g., HCPCS, GTIN, UNSPSC).

Because implementing content management service recommendations takes time, providers should make sure that they have the adequate staff resources before engaging a service.

If hospital leadership has decided to make this investment, they must be willing to establish processes for maintaining the integrity of the data that are accepted across the organization. If not, they may soon find themselves saddled with the same data chaos, creating an expensive and cumbersome cycle.

**BEST PRACTICE**

**Build interfaces between the hospital's systems**

Item master data can be combined with other sources to provide a comprehensive review of information, including the following:

- PO history, which provides insight into contracting opportunities as well as cases of rogue spending
- Accounts payable history, which provides insight into non-PO activity, such as purchased services
- Inventory reports, which provide insight into product use and ordering patterns, and help identify slow-moving or obsolete products

Hospital supply chain teams should work with their information technology colleagues and other key stakeholders to build links between the ERP, the chargemaster, the electronic health record (EHR), and any additional clinical information systems. The goal is to generate reports that illustrate the true cost of care and the relationship between supplies and clinical and financial outcomes. Remember, the item master should serve as the source of truth for supply information for all downstream systems.

*Explore the functionality of existing systems*

Taking the time to explore your hospital's existing MMIS or ERP functionality can be time well spent. Instead of investing in human capital to build interfaces, it is possible that your system can be upgraded to achieve the same goal.

In addition, hospitals may not be using the information in their existing systems to its full potential. Providers should explore whether their systems have the functionality to compare related supply costs and charges against reimbursement on an enterprise level in order to ensure that costs are adequately covered. Using pacemakers as an example, the questions below are the types of inquiries that should be made:

- How many different types of dual-chamber pacemakers are in the item master?
- What is the price for each type?
- Does the hospital's chargemaster reflect an appropriate charge for these pacemakers relative to their cost?
- Is there a significant price differential between vendors and types of devices? Are there separate chargemaster codes to reflect this?
- What is the expected reimbursement for these devices from each of the hospital's three largest payers?

An accurate item master generates more complete PO and expense information. In order to undertake any value-based initiative—looking at the cost per case and analyzing the connection between supply costs, use, and budget variances—organizations will need to link supply chain data with the general ledger; clinical information, operating room (OR), and procedural systems; and various other data sources. This integration will shine a light on the quality and accuracy of supply chain data. Maintaining a clean item master should be treated with the same level of importance as the maintenance of the organization's chargemaster.

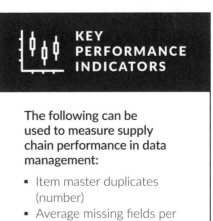

**KEY PERFORMANCE INDICATORS**

The following can be used to measure supply chain performance in data management:

- Item master duplicates (number)
- Average missing fields per item (%)
- PO items managed by item master (%)

Case Study

# Hartford HealthCare

**About Hartford HealthCare**

Hartford HealthCare is a fully integrated health system that includes a tertiary care teaching hospital, an acute care community teaching hospital, an acute care hospital and trauma center, two community hospitals, Connecticut's most extensive behavioral health network, a large multispecialty physician group, a regional home care system, an array of senior care services, a large physical therapy and rehabilitation network, and an accountable care organization. The Hartford HealthCare Cancer Institute provides coordinated care across five cancer centers and is a charter member of the Memorial Sloan Kettering Cancer Alliance.

In fiscal year 2016, Hartford HealthCare served 101 towns in its primary service area and had more than 370,000 emergency department visits, 370,000 primary care visits, and 400,000 acute care inpatient days annually. Hartford HealthCare employs more than 18,500 individuals.

**Background**

The Hartford HealthCare health system was created through strategic affiliations that stitched together a diverse group of previously autonomous healthcare providers. Each of five newly affiliated acute care hospitals had unique ERP and clinical information systems. Other providers that affiliated to form Hartford HealthCare's community network—including physician groups, senior care services, and rehab facilities—had smaller systems or manual processes, with limited technology platforms for supply chain functions. Those that had a system had individual item masters, charts of accounts, pricing files, and EDI connections—which created inefficiencies for collecting, maintaining, and monitoring data. There was no enterprise-wide data infrastructure and historical data was limited, ultimately rendering their reporting and analytics functionality inadequate. As Hartford HealthCare continued to mature and build its network by acquiring additional entities, the need for one ERP system—and a single source of truth for financial and supply chain data—became critical to building a foundation for integrating these new facilities into one common platform efficiently. Leaders across the organization needed more reliable information and they needed it faster.

Hartford HealthCare started with a clear set of strategic goals:

- Have one ERP system for the entire health system that would serve as the source of truth for data and one supply chain team at the corporate level. This team would be responsible for maintaining ERP data, with dedicated analysts responsible for adding and updating item and supplier information.
- Use a single set of item descriptions system-wide, with one ERP item number for each item (one item master shared across the entire health system for all acute care entities).
- Implement system-wide business processes to support data management.
- Align the procure-to-pay process across all Hartford HealthCare entities.
- Improve automation and efficiencies for the end users.
- Align procurement data with health records to support a clinically integrated approach to improving quality and reducing costs.

**Methodology**

Hartford HealthCare selected one ERP system to provide overall support for its facilities. It created a project team, including functional team leads, project management, change management, and training to ensure successful implementation in each institution and facilitate each go-live. A new cross-functional content management team comprising members from supply chain and finance was developed to maintain key data elements to support new business processes. Hartford HealthCare standardized policies, procedures, and business process workflows. Improvements to the new ERP system included the following:

- Partnering with suppliers for direct connection functionality to expand the item master without having to build and maintain the items
- Dramatically improving the number of EDI transactions for POs and invoices
- Real-time interface with clinical charging system
- Subscribing to modules for item cleansing and purchasing contract price management software to interface with the ERP system
- Establishing an ERP governance structure to monitor requests for ERP upgrades or enhancements
- Creating a standard process for onboarding new departments or entities—everyone follows the same model (e.g., automated dispensing technology for supplies and charging where applicable; inventory interfaces between procurement software and health records)

### Results

In 2015, Hartford HealthCare adopted a standardized procurement system at three acute care facilities, with all Hartford HealthCare entities scheduled to be on board by early 2018. One ERP system now supports the procure-to-pay business process, with flexibility to get additional entities on board using a consistent, coordinated approach. Hartford HealthCare moved from multiple acute care item masters to a single source of truth, which has further contributed to standardizing supplies. The single ERP system has improved efficiency by reducing off-contract spending, which has led to cost savings. Having the ERP system interface with its clinical system helps avoid discrepancies, further contributing to efficiency and smooth operation. Price negotiations and product recall support have been improved through the use of historical data. There is better communication and collaboration between system support departments, including accounts payable, purchasing, content management, finance, revenue cycle, and information technology services. The ERP system provides shared data, robust reporting, and analytic development. As Hartford HealthCare continues to build its operations using Lean principles (the system for creating more value using fewer resources), it will use this data to eliminate waste, increase capacity in its organization, and further enhance its business processes so that they are more efficient and customer-focused.

III.
──

# Creating a Standardized and Efficient Requisition Process

**CONTRIBUTORS**

Michael Berger | Ritika Ghose | Michael Jones | Dean Sheffield

A requisition is an official request for a product or service that arises out of a hospital need; it can be generated at any time by any authorized requester. But the way in which that request is handled can be critical to the hospital's bottom line. Imagine the financial impact if everyone in the hospital could simply call a supplier and order anything they felt they needed. Aside from the logistical challenges, hospitals would face a high volume of non-contracted spend (much of it through unapproved vendors) with no way to monitor spending activity.

Besides speed and efficiency, good requisitioning practices provide control of and visibility into spend. Linking requisitions to contracts helps to ensure that staff adhere to the item master. Hospitals and health systems should aim to create a centralized, automated requisitioning process that is funneled through purchasing and provides requisitioners with the information they need when they need it.

## BEST PRACTICE
**Have a standardized requisition process to eliminate rogue spending**
Standardization gives supply chain and finance staff greater control over financial resources. It also ensures that hospitals have a better idea of what is being

ordered and spent. The best way to eliminate rogue spending (circumventing the system) is to make certain that all requisitioners know how to place an order through the hospital's centralized process.

*Link requisition activity to the item master file*
To drive spend through the hospital's pre-approved item master (and eliminate rogue spending), try to make certain that requisitions only contain items that are in the item master. For electronic systems, this entails building an interface between the requisitioning platform and the system that houses the item master (if they are separate systems) so that a requisitioner who is making a purchase from an item master only needs to point and click a mouse. In hospitals that don't have an electronic requisitioning system, the paper requisition should contain a required field for the item master number. If no item master number is given, the requisition should be funneled through an approval process for off-contract items.

*Incorporate stock item master into requisition process*
Ideally, the replenishment of stock items is automated. If not, then in addition to linking requisition activity to the item master file, hospitals should ensure that both stock and non-stock items are requisitioned via the same process. For electronic systems, this entails linking the stock item file to the user platform whenever a requisition is created, then converting the stock requisition into a storeroom pick ticket rather than a non-stock PO. A pick ticket tells the inventory clerk which items and in what quantities to pick from the shelves for each department. Hospitals may also choose to prioritize stock items so that they appear above non-stock items in electronic searches. This helps drive requisition activity through the storeroom as much as possible, shortening the time between when the requisition is submitted and when the item is received. It can also help drive down the shipping costs associated with ordering non-stock items.

*Incorporate capital and purchased services into a centralized requisition process*
Spending associated with purchased services (linen and laundry, biomedical engineering, etc.) and capital equipment often falls outside of the supply chain purview. While the requisition process for these areas cannot be standardized in the same way that it is for medical/surgical items (mostly because the items being ordered cannot be included in the item master), it is still important to

have these requisitions go through the same channels in order to track spend and ensure that the requisitions are being reviewed and approved by the necessary parties.

*Establish punch-outs for non-medical/surgical items*

Many hospitals choose to standardize their requisition activities in such non-medical/surgical areas as information technology equipment, engineering, and office supplies by establishing punch-outs with contracted vendors. A punch-out is a portal to a vendor's website that is accessed through the hospital's electronic requisition system. A requisitioner initiates a requisition using the hospital's system,

## Use Clinician-Friendly Fields

It is important to include descriptor fields in requisiton forms that allow clinicians to identify the products they are requesting. For example, many clinicians refer to Y connectors as a "Christmas tree." Separate item and business description fields help supply chain personnel decipher what the requisitioner needs in cases where clinical jargon is often used.

which is automatically redirected to a catalog hosted by a specific vendor (e.g., an office supply vendor). Once the correct supply is identified from the catalog on the vendor site, the requisitioner submits the requisition to the hospital's purchasing department for PO creation and submission. Hospitals thus eliminate the need to incorporate these items in their item master, thereby cutting down on the overall maintenance required to keep the item master up-to-date. For hospitals that have an electronic system in place, punch-outs offer an easy way to standardize and streamline requisition activity for areas that typically fall outside of the supply chain purview.

*Create favorites lists*

Another way to streamline requisitioning is to build standardized favorites lists by user, service line, department, etc. A favorites list is a collection of frequently ordered items that can help drive uniform spending if managed effectively and also speed up the requisitioning process by eliminating the need for requisitioners to search for their items in the item master. Favorites lists are most commonly used with electronic procurement systems, but hospitals without electronic systems can still create, maintain, and distribute paper copies of favorites lists.

*Create templates*

People are more likely to adhere to a requisition policy when there are tools in place to help them. For hospitals that don't have electronic systems, templates are an effective way to standardize requisition content and make the process easier for end users. Create templates that list all the information needed to successfully complete a requisition, then make those templates readily available. Distribute paper copies to each unit and department or post a PDF on the hospital Intranet. Separate templates can be created for stock items and non-stock items. A fully completed form that includes all the required elements improves efficiency and ultimately saves time.

---

## Required Purchase Requisition Fields

- Requisitioner contact information
- Department
- Department/cost center number
- General ledger (expense) code
- MMIS number (if applicable)
- Vendor/manufacturer name
- Vendor/manufacturer part number

- Vendor/manufacturer contact information
- Item name and description
- Quantity
- UOM/quantity of each
- Unit price
- Total price
- Budgeted expense or non-budgeted expense

---

BEST PRACTICE

**Establish approval pathways for off-contract supplies**

For contracted supplies, many hospitals allow requisitions to flow through to purchasing without any approvals since the items being ordered have already been approved for purchase (ideally using value analysis). For off-contract purchases, it is important to balance the need for review with the equally important need for efficiency. Most hospitals structure the review requirements by spend authorization level (e.g., sometimes requisitions up to $5,000 require a director's signature, requisitions between $5,000 and $50,000 may require a director and an assistant vice president's signature, and so on). Regardless of the number of people a hospital designates as required approvers, it is most important to have and adhere to a predetermined approval process and timeline.

Requisitions that are created and reviewed electronically improve efficiency and accuracy. Automated systems typically incorporate a feature that alerts each reviewer (usually via email) when a requisition needs their signature.

**KEY PERFORMANCE INDICATORS**

**The following can be used to measure supply chain performance in requisitioning:**

- Preferred item requisitions (%)
- Requisition to PO (time)
- Electronic requisitions (%)
  - Percent electronic ÷ total requisitions
- Item master requisitions (%)
  - Percent of requisition line items with item master number

# IV

# Optimizing Purchasing Functions to Create Greater Operating Efficiencies and Cost Savings

CONTRIBUTORS

Michael Berger | Ritika Ghose | Michael Jones | Dean Sheffield

The challenging economic environment has led many hospitals and health systems to renew their focus on improving operating margins by reducing costs. The purchasing department frequently drives cost reduction and performance improvement initiatives. Purchasing serves as the liaison between requisitioning departments (most often clinical end users) and vendors. It is a core supply chain function that has greatly evolved from its transactional beginnings.

A purely transactional purchasing department takes requisitions from the ordering departments, follows up with specific requesters if any crucial information is missing, verifies contract coverage for requisitioned items, converts requisitions to POs, and dispatches those POs to the vendors (typically via EDI, email, phone, or fax). Purchasing is also responsible for following up with vendors about problematic POs. But as these transactional elements are automated via technology and streamlined through process coordination and standardization, purchasing departments are able to carry out more strategic activities.

### Verify contract coverage for product requests

When a requisition for a non-stock item or a purchased service has been submitted (and, if necessary, approved), purchasing should first determine whether the item is available through a contract. If it is not on contract, purchasing should then try to identify a functional equivalent that is on contract.

In purely transactional supply chains, purchasing manually verifies contracts for each order before the PO is created. However, there are significant efficiency gains to be reaped by automating this function. Most electronic requisition platforms can integrate item master and contract catalog content into the user interface, thereby driving requisitioners to select contracted items, which results in cost savings and increased efficiency because purchasing no longer has to verify contract coverage for these items. In fact, the majority of item master supplies do not need purchasing involvement at all, since everything has already been approved for ordering. In the most advanced supply chains, after appropriate approvals, these requisitions can be converted to POs automatically. Purchasing should strive to carry out manual contract verification and PO creation only for special requests (i.e., items that requisitioners order outside of the approved item master, which should represent a small percentage of overall order volume).

The more advanced requisition/content management systems can identify functionally equivalent items for non-contracted items, which is optimal, but purchasing should continue to work with the ordering department, contracting, and value analysis to determine whether the original item is truly needed. Items that are fully vetted by value analysis will then get incorporated into the item master and contract catalog. The next time they are ordered, there will be no need to get purchasing involved.

For true one-off items that lack a contracted functional equivalent, purchasing should see if the vendor is in the vendor master. Adding new vendors takes time and requires compliance review.

### Gather as much information as possible before processing orders

Purchasing must make certain that all of the information is accurate before placing an order for a special request. To avoid incurring unnecessary costs, ask the following questions:

- Did the requisitioner provide a written justification for the order?
- Do we need clinical input from end users?
- Did the requisitioner attach all necessary documentation (e.g., specifications)?
- If the requisitioner asks for overnight delivery, does the item truly require it?
- Does the requisition or contract cover all aspects of the total cost of ownership?

In the event that a different product is ordered (due to functional equivalence or because of policies established by the value analysis team), purchasing must also communicate that information back to the requistioner.

BEST PRACTICE
**Use data management to make purchasing more strategic**

*Automate purchasing through an EDI*
Technology—specifically an EDI—increases efficiency, reduces errors, and frees up time to focus on other purchasing issues. However, an EDI must be managed—ideally by purchasing. The setup involves boarding (entering) vendors into the EDI platform, which requires coordination between purchasing, the vendors, the EDI company, and other internal stakeholders. Advanced organizations regularly review potential vendors to board based on order volume. Some smaller vendors lack the necessary internal technology to participate in an EDI program, but most of the larger vendors (and all of the main distributors) have EDI capability.

*Address match exceptions*
When a PO is processed via an EDI portal, it is electronically routed directly to the vendor. Either the EDI or the vendor notifies purchasing about pricing, contract, or UOM issues, allowing purchasing to resolve match exceptions immediately. A match exception occurs when certain data elements (most commonly price, part number, or UOM) on a PO do not match the data that is stored in the vendor's system. Electronic ordering systems offer insight into occurrences of match exceptions, but it is up to hospital staff to resolve them. Many match exceptions related to contract pricing can result in improved MMIS data integrity, which is a step toward clean data and ensuring that

the right product is obtained at the right price. Match exceptions should be reviewed weekly at a minimum.

---

## Support the Procure-to-Pay Cycle

As organizations make strides in integrating key business processes across functional areas, the importance of a lean procure-to-pay cycle has become more apparent. The procure-to-pay cycle is the end-to-end process of ordering and obtaining supplies and remitting payment for them. Since reconciling contract price, PO price, and invoice price is so integral to this cycle, purchasing plays a vital part through its contract coverage and price verification process. The active role of purchasing in resolving match exceptions also prevents accounts payable discrepancies (instances where a hospital is invoiced at a price that is different than the PO price) by addressing the discrepancy as soon as it is submitted via the EDI.

---

BEST PRACTICE
### Support internal customers
When purchasing is responsive, answers questions, and provides support, internal customers are less likely to procure items outside of the defined approval channels.

Hospitals may want to consider assigning specific purchasing employees to specific product categories or service lines, which can improve relationships with both end users and vendors. This approach also helps purchasing staff develop greater expertise about their designated product category or service line.

The most strategic supply chains recognize purchasing as a repository of knowledge with subject matter expertise on a variety of areas, especially requisitioning. Not only does purchasing serve as the liaison between ordering departments and vendors, it often manages the requisitioner training program for both new and current requisitioners. Even though these professionals have different job functions, this arrangement makes sense because purchasing is the supply chain function with which requisitioners usually have the most interaction. At a minimum, new requisitioners should be required to undergo live or virtual training that incorporates the hospital's requisitioning process (policies, technology, best practices, etc.). All requisitioners should be given refresher training on a regular basis (at least once a year) to keep abreast of policy changes, technology updates, and more. In many cases, the supply chain department can help requisitioners understand what elements need to be in a contract, service-level agreements, delivery schedules, and other non-price elements.

## KEY PERFORMANCE INDICATORS

**The following can be used to measure supply chain performance in purchasing:**

- Exceptions (%)
  - Number of discrepant PO lines ÷ total PO lines
- Cost to issue a PO ($)
  - Annual supply chain department operating expense ÷ number of POs
- Automatic POs (%)
  - POs that automatically skip the buyer's desk
- POs through the EDI (%)
  - Total EDI POs ÷ total POs
- PO lines per full-time employee (number)

V.
—

# Enhancing the Receiving Process

CONTRIBUTORS

Michael Jones | Dean Sheffield

Receiving is the point at which a hospital takes physical possession of items typically procured via the purchasing process based on the terms and conditions of the PO. While this sounds straightforward—unload a truck and move items into the facility—the responsibility of receiving packages for a hospital can have both an immediate and a lasting financial impact.

The entire flow of receiving and distribution should be considered in concert and should incorporate steps to manage logistics.

BEST PRACTICE

**Make the best use of the space available**

Typically, the physical plant and property of a hospital are not modifiable, which may create receiving challenges that need to be addressed. Consider the following issues:

- Physical location of the facility
    - Is the hospital in an urban or non-urban setting?
- Access to the receiving area
    - Is the area dedicated to receiving activities?

- – Is it separate from other facility traffic?
- – Is the area completely contained on the facility's property?
- Size of receiving area
  - – What is the maximum length truck that can be accommodated?
  - – How many deliveries (i.e., trucks) can be accommodated at one time?
- Loading dock
  - – Is the loading dock a fixed height or variable from the ground?
    - › Is a truck lift gate required?
  - – What is the overhead clearance?
  - – How many unloading bays are available?
  - – What is the length and width of the loading dock?
  - – Is it dedicated exclusively to loading and unloading?
- Staging area
  - – Is it inside or outside?
  - – What is the size of the staging area?
  - – How far away is it from the loading dock?
  - – What is the access door clearance (length, height, width)?
- Receiving transaction area
  - – Is this area separate from the staging area?
  - – What is the size and location of the staging area?
- Predistribution area (location of received items prior to initial distribution)
  - – Is this area separate from the receiving area?
  - – What is the size and location of the predistribution area?
- Does the requisition or contract cover all aspects of the total cost of ownership?

BEST PRACTICE

## Establish a synergistic delivery schedule

One of the most important logistical considerations is delivery scheduling, which includes timing, phasing, and staging inbound freight. Business needs will most likely dictate the delivery schedule baseline, taking into consideration vendor volume and delivery frequency. Best practice is to partner with primary distribution and high-volume vendors to designate primary and secondary delivery schedules synergistically. Parcel vendors, such as FedEx® and UPS®, will need to be accommodated, most likely on a daily basis. It is also best practice to incorporate advance shipping notices to normalize the impact of non-routine deliveries, such as capital equipment.

In addition to enhancing the efficiency of receiving for the organization, creating a delivery schedule also benefits the carrier services and original supply vendors by standardizing the time they need on site to unload a truck. These efficiencies have a direct, positive impact on the finances of all parties involved.

The equipment required for receiving includes the following:
- Pallet jack (electric preferred)
- Hand trucks
- Carts (various sizes and configurations to meet business needs)
- Staging, receiving, and predistribution area shelving and racks
- Reusable pallets

BEST PRACTICE
### Have a standard procedure for validating items
Receiving is essentially validating deliveries, but it has several important components. The packages to be unloaded are matched to the shipping documentation (bill of lading, packing slip) and then typically cross-referenced to a facility PO. However, not all deliveries are originated by the hospital. Items may originate from vendors (whether or not they are associated with the hospital), field service engineers, or patients' family members. It is the responsibility of the receiving employee to determine the validity of the shipment and either reject or accept delivery. It is also important to have a policy in place for taking this decision to the appropriate person or department.

Primary distributors should provide an advanced shipping notice, which allows hospitals to electronically receive shipments, creating a more efficient process when products are physically delivered to the facility. There are myriad methods for electronic receiving (e.g., receive by exception); the best method is the one that works best for the institution and the technology and resources it has available.

Before the decision to accept a delivery is made, it is imperative that all items be thoroughly inspected. Once a delivery is accepted, the hospital may be contractually obligated to pay for the items. If no damage is noted upon inspection and damage goes undocumented by the carrier or vendor, the hospital may have limited recourse. When performed correctly, inspecting deliveries before accepting them mitigates the hospital's liability for damaged products and lowers the risk of disputes with vendors or carriers over damaged products.

For items associated with a PO, best practice is to match each line of the packing slip to the corresponding line on the PO and to officially receive the physical quantity that has arrived for each individual line. For items that are not associated with a PO, best practice is to log the delivery information. For example, if an item is delivered by FedEx, the FedEx tracking number should be logged to show the chain of custody through receiving.

As items are unloaded, they move to the staging area and are organized for physical receiving. Upon completion, items are further organized by final destination while they are still in the predistribution area. It is important to ensure that the integrity of the documentation is maintained at this juncture, which ties items to their final delivery location.

BEST PRACTICE
### Use strategic inventory management and distribution methods
Inventory management and distribution methods can influence the receiving process. They include the following:
- Low or logical unit of measure (LUM)
- Just-in-time (JIT) inventory
- Vendor-managed inventory (VMI)
- Consignment inventory
- Desktop delivery

LUM and JIT inventory are best practice strategies for reducing on-site inventory levels so that they meet real-time needs. They also reduce the frequency of supply replenishment (also known as inventory turns), which reduces inventory carrying costs. By eliminating excess stock on hand, these strategies also help minimize the waste associated with physically damaged items or packaging as well as the potential losses associated with products that have expired. Primary distribution partners typically offer these services. They incorporate the receiving separation process that is performed during traditional receiving and predistribution at the point of origin by grouping presorted items on carts with labeled destination areas.

The carts are then delivered directly to the predistribution area. Each facility needs to weigh the ROI associated with a LUM or JIT program, as the service may be subject to a distribution partner fee.

As its name indicates, in a VMI program the vendor completely manages its on-hand inventory at the hospital—from inventory counts to ordering to distribution. It requires a high level of understanding of the contractual responsibilities between the vendor and hospital. With a VMI program, the on-hand inventory is owned by the hospital.

A second option in VMI programs is the consignment model, where the on-hand inventory is not owned by the facility until it is used, at which time the hospital pays for the item.

Desktop delivery allows the vendor to bypass the traditional receiving processes and send packages right to the final location. Like VMI, desktop delivery relies on a high level of understanding between the involved parties. This model is often employed by office supply vendors.

The hospital's warehouse size and location may influence the use of all or some of the processes above. For example, a facility that doesn't have an on-site warehouse will typically embrace the LUM/JIT distribution partner process. This is a known best practice that transfers the holding cost of the warehouse inventory to the distribution partner, freeing both capital and storage space as well as streamlining receiving steps.

BEST PRACTICE
**Establish policies and procedures for special types of inbound and outbound freight**
There are certain situations that require specific procedures. Ensure that there are established ways to deal with special types of inbound freight, such as the following:

- Hazardous materials
- Frozen/refrigerated items
- Human tissue/bone products
- Biological products
- Pharmaceuticals

Policies and procedures should also be in place for handling direct deliveries for items that are not kept in stock and do not go through receiving (often referred to as a drop shipment). The supply chain can employ ERP technology to flag these instances and allow payments to be processed using a two-way match, in which a matching PO and invoice is required but not a receiving report in order for payment to be processed. This creates a much improved workflow down the line.

There should also be a process for item returns or mis-shipments.

**KEY PERFORMANCE INDICATORS**

**The following can be used to measure supply chain performance in receiving:**

- Electronic receiving (%)
  - Electronic receipts
    ÷ total receipts
- Invoice not received (%)
- Advance shipment notices (%)
  - Advance shipment notices
    ÷ total shipments

# VI.

—

# Taking a Holistic Approach
# to Distribution

CONTRIBUTORS

Michael Jones  |  Dean Sheffield

L ike receiving, distribution appears to be straightforward—take an item and deliver it. But make no mistake, delivery (or in its broader term, distribution) requires great preparation and attention to detail. An incorrect delivery impacts customer relations and increases the transaction cost. Therefore, distribution should be viewed holistically, including policies and the logistical steps for making a delivery.

BEST PRACTICE

**Foster a culture of constant customer service**

Distribution is a customer-facing supply chain activity that can profoundly influence customer relations (the customers being the individuals to whom the products are being delivered). Open, friendly customer service strategies are imperative to success and can be as simple as a warm greeting and open communications. Foster a service culture with distribution personnel by highlighting the importance of their role to the hospital. This practice also promotes collaboration and teamwork.

BEST PRACTICE

**Employ Lean principles in the predistribution area and delivery planning**

The handoff to distribution from receiving occurs in the predistribution area. This area should allow received items to be pre-staged and categorized into assigned zones or delivery locations. Make sure to have adequate storage and delivery carts or dollies available to meet the needs of the entire hospital. Further, care should be given to determining the area layout and flow in order to minimize bottlenecks. To meet these expectations, a best practice is to employ Lean principles, such as the following:

- Value stream mapping/analysis
  - Provides a visual representation of a workflow
- 5S: Sort, Set in Order, Shine, Standardize, Sustain
  - Simply stated, a place for everything and everything in its place
- Waste identification and remediation
  - Types of waste include the following:
    › Excess motion
    › Waiting
    › Reworking or excess movement of materials

The Theory of Constraints may be also applied. This five-step process for identifying the obstacles to achieving a goal is discussed in the chapter, "Realizing High Reliability Inventory Management."

BEST PRACTICE

**Develop delivery schedules and work assignments based on data**

Before creating delivery schedules and work assignments, consider the following questions:

- When do deliveries arrive?
- What days and times are they scheduled to be received?
- How long does receiving take to process a delivery?
- Are there advance shipping notices that may impact deliveries?
- Are there specific requirements set by the recipient (e.g., items must be delivered only during designated times)?

*Have personnel dedicated to specific delivery locations*

Having staff responsible for designated delivery locations provides consistency and helps build relationships between the supply chain and the delivery location personnel. Remember, distribution is customer-facing. To this end, it is also best practice to cross-train distribution staff to make certain that operations continue to run smoothly when someone goes on vacation, takes an extended leave, or resigns.

BEST PRACTICE

## Create a system based on the distribution model

When supplies are distributed they can originate from one of three locations: a warehouse, a procedural area, or the receiving dock. Depending on a hospital's available technology, physical layout, and human resources, each location requires a different internal distribution method that corresponds with the method used by the supply distributor. For example, if a hospital uses LUM or JIT inventory, supplies will be distributed from the receiving dock.

For each of these methods, the considerations for delivery include the following:

- The delivery documentation that indicates where items are to be delivered is attached to received items. This may be in the form of a paper proof of delivery that indicates the destination of the item or in an automated system.
- Proper modes of transport are employed (cart, dolly, or other defined means).
- Items are physically transported to the proper destination.
- The defined delivery confirmation is obtained.
- The delivery confirmation and the bill of lading/packing slip are maintained and filed per designated policy.

**KEY PERFORMANCE INDICATORS**

The following can be used to measure supply chain performance in distribution:

- Ad hoc deliveries (number)
  - Ad hoc deliveries to nursing floors or other areas

# NYC Health + Hospitals

**About NYC Health + Hospitals**

NYC Health + Hospitals is the largest public healthcare system in the U.S. It is a network comprising hospitals, post-acute/long-term care facilities, neighborhood health centers, nursing homes, and trauma centers. The system provides essential services to more than a million New Yorkers every year in more than 70 locations across the city's five boroughs.

**Background**

Historically, NYC Health + Hospitals operated as a set of independent entities loosely grouped into networks based on geography. Although each facility used the same materials management and financial systems, the item master content, contracting processes, and purchasing functions differed substantially across the enterprise. Beginning in 2009, NYC Health + Hospitals embarked on a project to implement an EDI platform and accompanying product suite across the health system as a means to standardize key supply chain functions, such as requisitioning, purchasing, contracting, and data management (specifically, management of item master content), as well as to gain greater visibility into spend and other key metrics through the platform's reporting tools.

Despite the efficiency gains achieved through this implementation, the resulting system architecture relied on disparate platforms strung together using interfaces, which limited the visibility of data and created redundant work, thus hampering NYC Health + Hospitals' ability to transform from a purely transactional supply chain to a strategic one. Moreover, although certain supply chain functions were standardized and (where possible) automated, the enterprise remained decentralized in key areas. Most urgently, NYC Health + Hospitals faces severe budget constraints year after year, necessitating major organizational transformation to reduce overall costs in both the short term and the long term.

NYC Health + Hospitals started with a clear set of strategic goals:
- Centralize purchasing and contracting
- Centralize item master content
- Launch value analysis
- Address supply chain process inefficiencies through short-term system enhancements and workarounds
- Reduce costs and track savings
- Implement an enterprise-wide ERP system to achieve long-term supply chain transformation

**Methodology**
Before embarking on specific process improvement initiatives, the health system centralized all of its purchasing and contracting staff and functions. Historically, each facility maintained its own purchasing team and often managed and negotiated contracts independent of the enterprise based on its own volume. In 2013, NYC Health + Hospitals moved its entire purchasing staff from their constituent hospitals spread out across New York City to a central office location in downtown Manhattan. It also reduced purchasing staff from 112 to 76 (staff members who chose not to relocate were transitioned to other roles within their specific hospitals). At the same time, all contracting responsibilities were transitioned to a central office sourcing team that developed and awarded contracts based on aggregated spend across the enterprise, with negotiated pricing extended to all facilities.

Also in 2013, NYC Health + Hospitals established one central, standardized item master for all facilities. It achieved this through a rigorous data review and normalization process to devise a single source of truth for both stock and non-stock items across the enterprise.

With key supply chain operational functions centralized, NYC Health + Hospitals was in a position to establish a more strategic process for contracting and incorporating new item master additions. In 2015, the health system launched a formal value analysis program for assessing supply spend, engaging clinical staff in strategy formation, tracking and validating savings, and creating organization-wide accountability. NYC Health + Hospitals launched a supply chain savings tracker of all its transactions, and booked successive savings/revenues of $10.5 million in fiscal year 2014, $24.3 million in fiscal year 2015, $39.9 million in fiscal year 2016, and $64 million in fiscal year 2017— validated by its finance department.

Although NYC Health + Hospitals had made great strides in establishing its overall supply chain as a strategic, integrated organization, the outdated system architecture resulted in an inefficient, purely transactional procure-to-pay process. Most notably, NYC Health + Hospitals faced a high volume of off-contract special purchase requests every month. They addressed this problem by establishing a comprehensive training program for all new and existing requisitioners, holding weekly OR focus group calls to explore additional contracting opportunities, and integrating punch-out catalogs for high-spend non-medical/surgical categories (such as engineering and information technology). The result was a 10% reduction in the monthly special purchase request rate.

NYC Health + Hospitals also faced a long requisition-to-PO cycle time, due to multiple (often redundant) approval and review steps, an uneven PO workload distribution for the purchasing staff, and a manual PO creation process. They addressed these inefficiencies by establishing formal guidelines for departmental requisition approval processes, reassigning POs to purchasing staff based on department (rather than based on requisitioner), and, most important, automating the PO creation process for orders that met certain eligibility requirements. This PO auto-approval program necessitated both a coordinated system enhancement of the procurement platform as well as a rigorous review of historical spend data to identify expense categories and product types that would be good candidates for program inclusion without negatively impacting operations.

The final and most far-reaching initiative was the implementation of an ERP system across the enterprise. This initiative kicked off in 2016 and is being rolled out in three-month waves, starting in July 2017 and running through June 2018. To ensure success, NYC Health + Hospitals established a full-time project committee, incorporating a content management team and a dedicated training team. They also worked closely with their implementation partner to ensure that the new system is configured appropriately to best address their business challenges. The guiding principles of the ERP project are to standardize, simplify, strengthen, and transform, all while gaining efficiencies and working on the broader goal to become more strategic.

## Results

In July 2017, NYC Health + Hospitals rolled out the majority of ERP finance modules as a single launch at all facilities and also launched supply chain modules (in concert with the accounts payable module) at two hospitals and in the central office. These latter rollouts will continue through June 2018 for all 21 facilities. As a result of the diligent work of the ERP project team, they have been able to take full advantage of a clean item master, enabling enhanced spend visibility. NYC Health + Hospitals has also been able to use the new ERP system to further drive the process improvement initiatives already underway, most notably reducing off-contract spend, shortening the procure-to-pay cycle time enhanced by the automated three-way match, and decreasing PO exceptions. NYC Health + Hospitals is also availing itself of the automation capabilities of the ERP to fully revamp its distribution model, moving away from bulk distribution in favor of JIT/LUM distribution via a two-bin replenishment system. (Further information about a two-bin system is included in the "Realizing High Reliability Inventory Management" chapter.) This revised distribution model is being rolled out over 30 months, beginning in November 2017. Through all the efficiency gains enabled by the ERP and the processes built to support the successful implementation of the system, NYC Health + Hospitals forecasts a savings of over $100 million in fiscal year 2018 with continually escalating savings through fiscal year 2020.

# VII

# Realizing High Reliability Inventory Management

CONTRIBUTORS

Michael Jones | Robert Rizzi | Kenneth Scher | Dean Sheffield

Inventory management is the process of administering the hospital's expendable assets. For the healthcare supply chain, those assets are the supplies necessary to run healthcare operations and deliver patient care. Hospital stakeholders often view inventory management as the main—if not sole—function of the supply chain department, as clinicians rely on supply chain staff to make sure that patient care products are in the right place at the right time. There are myriad challenges involved in achieving best practice inventory management. The manner in which every supply and its associated value are managed can significantly impact a hospital's operational efficiency, financial performance, and care quality.

In the past, inventory management addressed individual aspects as opposed to taking a holistic approach to problem-solving. Today's supply chain professionals must go beyond resolving issues on a day-to-day basis and focus on how to make their facility a high reliability organization (HRO). The HRO approach focuses on 1) preoccupation with failure, 2) resisting the temptation to simplify observations, 3) sensitivity to operations, 4) commitment to resilience, and 5) regard for expertise.[1] Applying HRO values to managing hospital inventory can help prevent obstacles from arising in an environment where undesirable situations are likely to occur, due to the high number of risk factors.

In inventory management, numerous factors involve other supply chain areas, which can have a ripple effect on downstream operations. For one, inventory management controls and processes must be applied from the moment products arrive on the receiving dock in order to ensure that there is an accurate record of products on hand. Then there are the risks associated with product demand, seasonality, item backorders and allocations, technology, and so on that directly impact requisitioning. Specific to inventory management are anticipating demand and the calculations associated with inventory replenishment—as well as handling specialty items, especially those for the perioperative and procedural hospital units.

## HRO 101

Even small mistakes can lead to great harm in the complex world of healthcare. Relative to inventory management, patient care can suffer if a surgeon or clinician doesn't have the right product at the right time or an intensive care nurse can't find a needed supply quickly. The high reliability concept must be adapted to an organization's culture, operations, and technology infrastructure in order to be most effective. The tenets of a culture focused on continuing process improvement (see "The Fundamentals" chapter) are particularly applicable here.

Traits of HROs:
1. **Preoccupation with failure:** HROs destigmatize failure. Employees are encouraged to consider ways—both large and small—in which their work processes might fail and then share those thoughts with superiors. This supports implementing safeguards.
2. **Resisting the temptation to simplify observations:** HROs emphasize finding the true underlying source of a problem rather than settling for broad explanations. Organizations are more successful if they ask questions and solve real issues.
3. **Sensitivity to operations:** An HRO workforce is keenly aware of how processes affect operations. In a transparent environment, this attention to detail leads to observations that drive better decision-making and workflow.
4. **Commitment to resilience:** HROs are prepared to respond to failures, as their employees are skilled problem-solvers who are committed to finding solutions.
5. **Regard for expertise:** This involves listening to those who have the most knowledge about the task at hand. This is especially true of HRO leaders—they listen to and respect the input of their staff, regardless of seniority.[2]

The key components of inventory management include locations (the main storeroom or unit-specific locations), cycle counting (a count of every product found in all locations, accomplished by continuously selecting smaller portions of inventory to count throughout a select time period for the purpose of validation and replenishment), and periodic automatic replenishment (PAR) levels (the maximum and minimum quantities of a specific product that should be kept in a certain location). These components are influenced by internal and external stakeholders, institutional culture, and technology. For example, clinicians are the largest internal stakeholders, as they determine the need for patient supplies, while vendors are external stakeholders, as they provide supplies. A hospital culture that supports multidisciplinary collaboration and educates clinicians about the methodology behind inventory management fosters a more efficient environment, reduces costs, improves morale, and enhances the quality of care throughout the facility. This is particularly important in the OR—frequently the hospital's highest revenue-generating department. All supply chain executives should strive to use technology and be able to automate the main components of inventory management. Supply chain leaders would do well to consider technology solutions to enhance their ERP or MMIS and provide insight into how products are being used in other areas of the hospital. Technology offers the controls, data, and reporting needed to improve performance and better control costs in an area that has a direct impact on care delivery and the hospital's bottom line.

Even with limited resources, inventory management professionals can lower costs and improve organization-wide quality and operations by implementing best practices. There is a great deal to consider. This chapter focuses on the basic best practices for achieving a well-functioning inventory management system.

## The Cornerstone of Inventory Management

The item master is the main source of inventory management data. That's why item master data must be clean in order to achieve best practice inventory management. Data management is the cornerstone of inventory management. It feeds information inward and outward from each of its components to drive decision-making.

## Have an inventory control strategy

The way in which a hospital's supplies are maintained largely depends on the facility size, the patients served, the number of units or floors, and the technology in place. It also depends on the hospital's distribution model (whether it is LUM, JIT, or bulk).

Besides the main storeroom, there are unit-specific storerooms, which are often referred to as PAR locations. Inventory strategies that can be applied to these locations include the following:

- Simple storage: The use of item locations and bins as well as bar code technology, if available.
- Two bin: A method that uses two bins; an empty bin signals the need for replenishment. The first is taken away to be refilled and the second is pulled forward.
- Exchange carts: A full cart of items is delivered to each location and exchanged for the empty one that is currently there.
- Technology can be used to enable inventory replenishment, such as weight scales and radio frequency identification (RFID).

Varying factors determine the best strategy for hospital PAR locations. The most important thing is to ensure that only one inventory strategy is used for all PAR locations across the organization. Measures can also be taken to arrange unit-specific storerooms so that they provide a better workflow.

*Group items by type, frequency of use*

The following should be applied as general best practice, but environmental requirements should be considered depending on the type of storage (clean, sterile, etc.).

The items that are used constantly should be stored in a primary reach area (i.e., within arm's length) so that staff don't have to bend down or use a step stool to get them. Limiting the need to bend down or get a step stool saves time and reduces the risk of worker injury. Keep items that are used for similar tasks near each other. For example, group bins that contain personal hygiene items for patients in one area and items that are needed to dress wounds in another area. It will make it easier to pull related items without having to go around the storeroom to find them all. It is best practice to design each unit-specific storeroom in the same way to support floating nurses and physicians. Make sure clinicians, including new hires, are familiar with the layout.

*Use labeled bins to hold items in unit-specific storerooms*
Only store one type of item per bin (e.g., do not put 5% dextrose solution and 10% dextrose solution in a single bin). When a bin contains more than one type of item, especially if the items are similar in shape, there is a greater risk of slowing down the process because the staff member must double-check that the correct item has been pulled. Mixing items also increases the risk of distributing the wrong item when staff is in a hurry or, in the unit-specific storeroom, the risk of clinical staff picking the wrong item.

The front of each bin should have a label for the product it contains that includes the following information:

- Item location: This is the bin number or nomenclature so that staff can find it more quickly. If an electronic system is used, the item location should be included.
- Item part number: Both the manufacturer and distributor/vendor item numbers should be listed, as sometimes orders must be placed through the manufacturer.
- Item description: This helps ensure that the correct item is pulled. Instead of just pulling an item from bin 19, for example, staff can confirm that the item pulled from bin 19 is exactly the item that has been requested.
- Item master file number: This is an important internal tracking number that the hospital can use to measure the amount of spend in a particular area and optimally link the product to patient outcomes, such as readmissions.
- Minimum and maximum amounts: These should be based on the purchase UOM: does the item get purchased in a box or individually (i.e., each)? The associated UOM ensures accuracy and provides context.
- Bar codes: If the hospital has the technological resources, they can include bar codes on bins to provide a scan that matches the information above to the item that has been requested, which improves workflow.

Mark all bins with a number or other nomenclature. Keep on hand a map of the bin locations, their identifying numbers, and their contents so that inventory management and other staff can locate them quickly. For example, if a unit has requested alcohol pads, instead of an employee having to look in each bin, the inventory management system shows the exact bin it is in.

*Follow The Joint Commission and departments of health requirements for organizational environment and layout*
The Joint Commission has specific requirements about where shelving should be placed: 18 inches below the ceiling fire sprinklers and six inches off the floor to protect items from flooding. Bottom shelves should also have splash guards to protect the supplies from flooding or dirt kicked up from the floor. Check and enforce all government requirements and those of any accrediting body.

*Keep hard-copy backups*
Make sure that there are hard copies of PAR sheets, bin labels, and policies and procedures for easy reference in the event of a power outage or technology system failure. When training inventory management staff, make sure everyone knows where to find these hard copies.

### BEST PRACTICE
## Examine inventory cycle for constraints

Inventory management can identify and improve workflow problems by applying the Theory of Constraints, which was developed by Eliyahu Goldratt to help managers make changes to business systems. Goldratt's theory envisions that a system (such as inventory management) is made up of linked activities that create a chain and, much like the adage, the weakest link in that chain limits the rest of the system. Finding that system constraint (as he calls it), and focusing on improving that bottleneck improves the overall system.

The methodology is made up of the following steps:
- Identify the constraint.
- Exploit the constraint with existing resources.
- Subordinate and synchronize the constraint by reviewing all other activities in that system chain to ensure that they are in alignment with and support the needs of the constraint.
- Improve performance of the constraint. If it has not improved, consider what else needs to be done to fix it. Capital investment may be required.
- Repeat the process.

Goldratt also describes the types of constraints an organization may face when trying to improve a system:

- Physical constraints, which can include material shortages, a lack of space, or a lack of staff.
- Policy constraints, which may involve current facility policies and procedures or regulatory requirements being at odds with industry best practices. Such constraints can also take the form of new employees being informally trained in procedures that are not best practice.
- Paradigm constraints, which are deeply engrained beliefs and habits that are difficult to change (the mentality of "We have always done it this way—why do we have to change?").
- Market constraints, which is when production capacity exceeds sales or the external marketplace is constraining throughput. In inventory management, product shortages are a market constraint.

BEST PRACTICE
### Use cycle counts to track inventory in unit-specific locations
Cycle counts involve reviewing the contents of a bin to 1) verify the information in the electronic system and 2) know when a product needs to be replenished. Set aside time to count one section of the storeroom each week. If discrepancies are discovered, perform a root cause analysis to identify the issue. Even if inventory management can demonstrate that a cycle count has been conducted each week for a year and those amounts have consistently matched, an annual physical inventory count may still be required.

*Use a perpetual inventory model for main storeroom and high-value areas*
Perpetual inventory is an electronic method that tracks all receipts and issues (disbursements) and maintains an active dollar value and count of product on hand in real time. This model is useful within procedural areas (such as the OR) to track items that move quickly through a particular department/area (e.g., endomechanicals). This creates a more efficient replenishment process.

BEST PRACTICE
### Rotate stock to avoid expiration and waste
Inventory management analytics let staff see where products are being used and how frequently. This can help reduce the likelihood that an item will expire,

lose sterility, or be damaged before it can be used.

While analytics can help identify places or times when more or fewer items are needed, the inventory management department must also be flexible, due to the ever-changing conditions in hospitals. For example, during the avian influenza outbreak, a greater demand for personal protection devices (N-95 masks, barrier protection) significantly changed stock patterns and quantities. Similarly, an unusually dangerous virus such as Ebola can dramatically change the quality and level of personal protective equipment requirements for patient care, including the use of powered air purifying respirators (PAPRs).

*Establish PAR levels*

To ensure that products are available when they are needed, hospitals need to establish PAR levels so that supplies are reordered in a timely manner and the hospital doesn't run out of essential patient care items. The following factors must be considered when determining PAR levels to help keep inventory flowing smoothly throughout the hospital:

- Use
  - UOM/quantity of each
- Lead time
  - When calculating PAR levels for each item, make sure a reorder point is established that incorporates the lead time required for ordering that product. It will help guarantee that enough of the item is always available.
- Operating inventory
  - How many days' worth of inventory is it necessary to have on hand?
- Safety stock
  - It is important to plan ahead so that stock is always available when needed. For example, holidays or bad weather (both near the hospital itself and elsewhere) can delay or disrupt shipping and deliveries. It might be prudent to order more than usual the week before holidays or in advance of anticipated bad weather events.

PAR levels should not be static. They should be reviewed consistently to avoid the effects of seasonality, patient mix, item changes, backorders, etc. A hospital isn't a static environment and PAR levels must reflect that. When determining reorder points, never allow any item to drop to the point where there is only one in the building. Following HRO principles, the inventory management team should be preoccupied with failure—which, in this case, means running out of product. There should be a process to determine how much of an item should always be kept in stock.

**KEY PERFORMANCE INDICATORS**

**The following can be used to measure supply chain performance in inventory management:**

- Storeroom average days on hand (number)
  - Storeroom inventory value ÷ annual distribution spend
- OR average days on hand (number)
  - OR inventory value ÷ annual OR spend
- Annual stock outs (number)
- OR inventory value ($)
  - OR inventory value ÷ number of rooms

1. M.R. Chassin and Loeb, J.M., "High-Reliability Health Care: Getting There from Here," *The Milbank Quarterly* vol. 91, no. 3 (2013); 459-490.
2. Gamble, M., "5 Traits of High Reliability Organizations: How to Hardwire Each in Your Organization," *Becker's Hospital Review*, (April 2013). https://www. beckershospitalreview.com/hospital-management-administration/5-traits-of-high-reliability-organizations-how-to-hardwire-each-in-your-organization.html (accessed August 30, 2017).

Case Study

# Kaleida Health

### About Kaleida Health

Kaleida Health is the largest healthcare provider in Western New York, with four acute care hospitals that have more than 1,000 beds, two long-term care facilities, a visiting nurse service, and more than 80 clinics throughout its hospitals and the region. Kaleida Health hospitals see more than one million patients each year.

### Background

Kaleida was losing a significant amount on expired inventory each year, due to a process that required staff to review supply levels manually and place bulk orders. Further, nurses or billing staff had to review patient charges and supplies used daily, record the information on a paper form, and manually submit the charges for payment. These two manual processes resulted in excessive inventory and caused delays to posting patient charges. Kaleida wanted to reduce the number of supplies that went unused before their expiration date and create a process that allowed nurses to spend more time caring for patients rather than managing supplies.

### Methodology

Kaleida adopted an automated replenishment program that uses bar codes to replenish supplies through clinical documentation. The hospital system formed a multidisciplinary, system-wide team, including the director of materials management, representatives from clinical and financial departments, information services and technology, and nurses who coordinated the charge capture, purchasing, and chargemaster functions. The team holds weekly meetings and reports to a steering committee and the chief financial officer quarterly.

Using ERP software, disposable supply items were given a materials management number and bin location in order to identify them and their respective department locations individually. Manufacturer bar codes were scanned into the ERP system; each item was verified by purchasing and the finance team. The materials management team sets the reorder, minimum, and maximum quantities in a perpetual inventory system. Now, when an item reaches its minimum level, the system determines if the product resides at another site and has not been used in 45 days. If so, the product is placed in a "no move" report (indicating that it is not to be taken off the shelf to be used in a procedure or another area) and then sent to the requesting location. If the item is not available, a PO is created to replenish the maximum level.

The information services and technology team created an item master replication process that sends extracted ERP data for clinical support review and is then entered into the chargemaster software. The chargemaster software compares its information with the extracted data and makes updates daily.

Materials management physically counts inventory and enters the counts into the ERP system so that a report will show the supplies that will be ordered that day. The report is reviewed to ensure that the correct amount of product is ordered and to determine whether any product needs expediting. Orders are then sent electronically to purchasing and then to the supplier.

Nurses document the supplies used for each patient by scanning the bar code for each item. If items lack a bar code, Kaleida creates one. Common, low-cost medical/surgical items, such as bandages and gauze, are not part of the automated replenishment program. The bar code system charges products and debits inventory without human intervention, and provides a daily report that identifies any inconsistencies or insufficient quantities.

### Results

Kaleida named their program e2, which stands for Elimination of Expired Product. By keeping staff educated about e2, they have reduced the number of expired products in the ORs, improved patient safety, and improved accreditation compliance.

Kaleida has implemented this process in 16 departments, including ORs and cath labs. It has led to 100% accuracy on charge codes, which helps ensure accurate billing. Not a single case has been canceled due to missing items. The automated replenishment program helps materials management rotate items to make sure that they are used before their expiration date, which has saved Kaleida more than $50,000 annually. Each department has reduced the percentage of on-hand inventory it carries compared to revenue. The automation also allows materials management to focus on total supply chain management and strategic decision-making. Importantly, nurses now spend less time locating and documenting the supplies used and spend more time with patients.

Case Study
————————

# Hospital for Special Surgery

**About Hospital for Special Surgery**

Hospital for Special Surgery (HSS) is the world's leading academic medical center focused on musculoskeletal health. HSS is nationally ranked number one in orthopedics and number three in rheumatology by *U.S. News & World Report* (2017-2018), and is the first hospital in New York State to receive Magnet Recognition for Excellence in Nursing Service from the American Nurses Credentialing Center four consecutive times. HSS performs more than 30,000 surgical procedures annually and has one of the lowest infection rates in the country. HSS is an affiliate of Weill Cornell Medical College, and as such all HSS medical staff are faculty of Weill Cornell. The hospital's research division is internationally recognized as a leader in the investigation of musculoskeletal and autoimmune diseases. HSS has locations in New York, New Jersey, and Connecticut.

**Background**

There are a vast number of implant types. To manage its specialized inventory for hip, knee, and spinal implant surgeries, HSS operates two storeroom locations that are dedicated to orthopedic implants. The hospital has approved and maintains inventory for a number of arthroplasty implant systems that satisfy specific patient needs and surgeon preferences. Individual implant systems can have numerous individual components, and individual components can come in a variety of sizes. For example, femur implants alone come in over 20 different lengths and diameters; patellas come in over 30 different sizes. Ensuring that the hospital has the correct implant in the correct size at the required time while simultaneously balancing the facility's limited storage space has been a significant challenge.

HSS's implants are made available on a consignment basis, allowing vendors to leave a certain number of implants at the hospital but charging only for those that are used. This is a particularly important cost management solution, as HSS does not bear the expense of the inventory investment nor the risk that the items will expire prior to being used. Managing the inventory was a labor-intensive process in which staff manually monitored product expiration dates; determined how many implants remained on the shelf; tracked backorders and backorder issues; figured out what stock was on hand during surgery, after surgery, and in preparation of next-day cases; and finally, placed orders via paper requisitions, making it difficult to keep track of POs and backorders.

HSS surgeons identify the implant system that will be required when a case is scheduled. The implant room is responsible for ensuring that all necessary implants are available on the day of surgery. The case will not start until implant availability is confirmed, underscoring the importance of having an extremely accurate inventory management system.

As HSS expanded its OR capacity, the number of surgeons, and the number of approved vendors, it became clear that their manual process for managing inventory would no longer suffice. With over 12,000 different implants in the implant room (the vast majority of which have expiration dates), keeping track of inventory manually proved to be a monumental task.

## Methodology

HSS leadership decided to install a materials management software system that tracks available and used implants, including quantities, lot number, expiration date, and inventory locations. The system also automates reordering of implants used and is interfaced with the hospital's MMIS.

As a means of enhancing patient safety and OR efficiency, the hospital implemented an implant verification system that was developed by an HSS surgeon and a software expert. It has the ability to scan implants prior to their introduction into the sterile field. It determines the compatibility of various components, the correct laterality, and makes certain that the product has not expired. This information, along with lot or serial number, is also entered into the patient's EHR for future reference.

The hospital's implant technicians received extensive training on the materials management software, which encompassed scanning items in and out of inventory, receiving items in the system, and tracking and ordering implants. Clinical staff were also trained on the implant verification software, as it is predominantly used by their team as well as in the OR.

## Results

The implementation of materials management software and implant verification software has helped the inventory management staff better track what has been used, leading to fewer instances of implants needed for surgery not being available. The software programs have also helped improve OR efficiency and ultimately patient care. Now the circulating nurse scans all arthroplasty implants into the implant verification software prior to opening the packages. Once the nurse has scanned the implants, the software verifies that the implants supplied for cases are compatible, have correct laterality, and have not expired.

The materials management software has also led to fewer discrepancies during vendor consignment audits that ensure that HSS is accountable for all implants that are supplied to them and used on patients.

HSS is currently working with the developer of the implant verification software to develop and implement additional functionality that will help predict implant sizes needed prior to the day of surgery and will automate the process of requesting implants from the implant room. These changes will further improve patient safety and the efficiency of a very busy OR.

# Operating at the Intersection of Cost, Quality, and Outcomes

# VIII

# Capturing and Applying Alternative Data Sets

CONTRIBUTORS

Jeffrey Ashkenase | Ritika Ghose | Martin Glick | Perry Sham | Bruce Vladeck, PhD

Understanding total costs is essential to managing any aspect of a hospital successfully. Supply chain represents a significant portion of hospital expenditures (second only to payroll) and must take responsibility for evaluating its performance compared to the organization's financial goals. When evaluating total costs, it is important to tie costs to the actual hospital "products"—namely, patient stays. Hospital finance departments are increasingly classifying patient stays as a mixture of clinical conditions and the treatment provided for those conditions. For every hospital product (patient stay/clinical condition/treatment), there is supply consumption. The supply chain is responsible for the components of total supply expense.

Hospital finance is complicated and multi-layered. Therefore, it can be very challenging for a health system to assess whether reimbursement covers the cost of treatment on a patient level. There are a variety of reasons for this, including the fact that not every supply used to treat a patient is associated with the patient encounter. This makes the supply chain's ability to tie actual supply costs to revenue difficult and often fruitless.

Health systems always aim to provide the highest quality of care. In a value-based environment, it is also in their best financial interest to do so. The metrics

**The Components of Total Supply Expense (under supply chain purview)**

1. Cost of supplies/services: Ensuring that (wherever possible) supplies are covered under a contract, ordered on a PO, and ordered at the lowest price.
2. Availability of supplies: Ensuring that the necessary products are available for use when needed and that inventory levels are at optimal levels to minimize stock-outs, shrinkage, and obsolescence.
3. Quality of supplies: Ensuring that the products used by the facility are the appropriate quality for their intended use.
4. Identifying the impact of supplies on patient care.

that are traditionally used to evaluate supply chain—principally *supply expense per adjusted acute discharge, supply expense per adjusted acute patient day, supply expense as % of net patient revenue,* and *supply expense as % of total operating expense*— do not accurately measure supply chain efficacy because they depend on factors outside the sphere of supply chain. Further, whether used as a single metric or as a component of a larger dashboard, these metrics don't address a facility's effectiveness at improving quality and outcomes. In fact, inaccurate conclusions may be reached about an organization's performance by using only the current metrics (and only focusing on the cost component). A facility perceived as a high performer may be achieving success at the expense of quality and outcomes. Similarly, an institution perceived as a high-cost, low performer may be doing so in order to achieve higher quality and, consequently, better outcomes.

Clearly, a different method of measurement is required. Familiarizing the supply chain with alternative data sets that identify the correlation between supplies and clinical outcomes, thus providing greater clarity about which supply chain areas can strategically contribute to improved organizational performance in a value-based environment, is an essential step toward operating at the intersection of CQO.

BEST PRACTICE

**Familiarize the supply chain with a new suite of metrics**

New data sets should be used to evaluate the effectiveness of the supply chain in addressing organizational cost, quality, and outcomes. Each metric should be chosen based on a clinical condition that is strongly influenced by the use of supplies. While a lack of data has historically been a barrier to developing these types of metrics, the data collection infrastructure and reporting mechanisms that the CMS has encouraged hospitals to adopt offer a new platform to use for these purposes. For example, if relevant data related to central line-associated bloodstream infections (CLABSIs) is already being collected by quality and infection control personnel, the supply chain can also use this information to evaluate how products may be affecting the outcomes of those procedures.

Examples of clinical conditions and outcomes where supply chain may have an impact include the following:
- Reduction in catheter-associated urinary tract infections (CAUTIs)
- Reduction in all pressure ulcers (Stage III and IV)
- Reduction in vascular catheter-associated infections (CLABSIs, etc.)
- Reduction in surgical-site infections (e.g., following bariatric surgery, certain orthopedic procedures, and mediastinitis after coronary artery bypass grafting)
- Reduction in certain types of falls and trauma
- Foreign object retained after surgery
- Medication errors
- Patient death or serious injury associated with the use of contaminated drugs, devices, or biologics provided in the healthcare setting
- Patient death or serious injury associated with the use or function of a device in patient care, in which the device is used for functions other than as intended
- Patient death or serious injury associated with unsafe administration of blood products
- Patient death or serious injury associated with the use of restraints or bedrails while being cared for in a healthcare setting

Because these metrics evaluate outcomes that span multiple patient types, it may be appropriate to segment outcomes by patient care unit (e.g., critical care, medical/surgical, cardiac), patient type (surgical, medical, etc.), or specific procedure. This may require sub-reports.

The best way for the supply chain to collect this information is to build a link between its data (through an MMIS or ERP) and the organization's EHR. As referenced in the "Using Sound Data to Measure Performance and Support Value-Based Initiatives" chapter, this provides the supply chain with a better method for extracting and analyzing data to drive evidence-based purchasing decisions.

## Monitor the quality of new product alternatives

It is important to monitor the quality of new product alternatives to determine if they are of equal or better quality (e.g., reduce infections, reduce length of stay, are easier for clinicians to use) than the products being used. For example, while the use of a silver alloy urinary (Foley) catheter may reduce the incidence of CAUTI, it is important to monitor its failure rate and compare it to historical silicone or latex catheter failure rates. This could be monitored through the measurement of an "input divided by output" metric intended to calculate the yield (failure) rate per outcome. In the example of CAUTI, this could be calculated as follows: *(silver catheter use ÷ discharges where urinary catheter was inserted) – historic rate (non-silver catheter use ÷ discharges where urinary catheter was inserted)*.

## Evaluate performance and create dashboards

Traditional methods of analyzing supply chain metrics focus on a comparison of a facility's performance against a peer group to determine whether they are performing favorably or unfavorably. While it is valid to compare performance against peers, organizations should first aim to trend performance internally (due to the early stages of the metrics being proposed). Once the criteria for determining peer groups have been decided and the guidance for determining the appropriate source of underlying data has been decided, then it may be appropriate to evaluate the organization against its peers.

Evaluating a hospital's performance against itself can be accomplished in the following manner:

Incident Rate

Establish a lower (where the hospital wants to be) and upper (the highest level that the hospital is willing to accept) boundary of performance. The lower boundary should be the targeted incident rate set by the facility. In the case of a "never event" (medical errors that should never occur), such as a foreign object retained after surgery, the target may be zero. However, in the case of less serious outcomes, such as a CAUTI, a value that is low but higher than zero may be appropriate. The upper boundary should be the highest acceptable incident rate a facility is willing to accept. This may change over time as new products and procedures are introduced into the process. The performance during each period is relative to the upper and lower boundaries.

- *performance > upper boundary:* Red
- *performance < upper boundary but > lower boundary:* Yellow
- *performance ≤ lower boundary (performance = lower boundary where the lower boundary is zero):* Green

Cost Measures (Output Measure and Opportunity Cost Per Outcome):
The measures can be compared against historical averages to gauge performance, such as the average of three preceding months.

- *performance > x% average preceding 3 months:* Red
- *performance ≤ x% average preceding 3 months:* Yellow
- *performance < average preceding 3 months:* Green

It is important to recognize—and make clear to internal stakeholders and leadership—that even for outcomes that have a supply component, supplies are just that—*a component* that can contribute to the success or failure of an outcome. The human element, such as how the supplies are being used in accordance with evidence-based best practices, should be considered the chief driver in quality and outcome improvement. To this end, a multidisciplinary team that holds all stakeholders accountable should evaluate outcomes-based metrics. In addition to supply chain, this team should include clinical and operational leadership as well as physicians, nursing, quality, and infection control personnel.

In order to provide key facility stakeholders with a more comprehensive view of performance across all of the outcomes being monitored, metrics can be summarized as an executive dashboard. The average performance for the two cost measures noted in this chapter (*supply expense per volume* and *opportunity cost per outcome*) can be combined to calculate a consolidated cost measure evaluation. Given the larger financial impact associated with outcomes versus supply expense, it may be desirable to calculate a weighted average of the two metrics, giving higher weight to the *opportunity cost per outcome.*

Combining the incident rate and cost metrics determines if a facility is highly effective, moderately effective, or ineffective. The overriding metric is the incident rate. A facility scoring green in the incident rate category is deemed to be highly effective. The degree to which it is highly effective is determined by its performance in the cost metric. Thus, a facility could be highly effective based on their outcomes, but in the third degree of performance based on their cost metrics. Ideally, facilities want to have a low incident rate while also being a low-cost provider. However, it may be necessary to increase costs to achieve these outcomes. The worst-case scenario is having poor outcomes (ineffective) while also being a high-cost provider.

## Hospital-Acquired Catheter-Associated Urinary Tract Infections (CAUTIs)

Let's use the example of CAUTI to demonstrate how the supply chain can use alternative data sets to analyze the relationship of supply costs to quality and outcomes.

### OUTPUT MEASURE

Output measures are the prevalent metrics that are used to evaluate supply chain where supply expense is compared against a measure of volume, such as *adjusted acute discharges* or *adjusted acute days*. While this metric should not be the only measurement, it is a useful indicator in a larger evaluation. The output metric in this example would be *supply expense per discharge where a urinary catheter was inserted*. Under the current method of evaluating this metric, optimally it should be as low as possible, with an expected downward trend over time to reflect performance improvement. But when accounting for quality and outcomes, this metric may increase, decrease, or remain unchanged over time. The best case scenario is when quality and outcomes measured are optimized.

### OUTCOMES/OUTPUT MEASURE (INCIDENT RATE)

This metric measures the undesired outcome against the potential population that could experience the outcome. Continuing with our example, we would use *number of CAUTIs ÷ discharges where urinary catheter was inserted*. This metric would provide a rate of undesired outcomes, which are expected to trend downward over time, with the ultimate goal being a zero rate of occurrence.

### OPPORTUNITY COST OF OUTCOMES MEASURE

This metric measures the monetary impact associated with the undesired outcome. This impact may either be an increase in cost (the cost associated with additional procedures, longer average length of stay, etc.) or decrease in revenue (penalties, denied claims, outlier payments, etc.). For the CAUTI example, calculate *cost of outcomes + penalties ÷ incidences of CAUTI*. Once again, a downward trend would be expected over time, optimally with a zero opportunity cost.

The significant shift is that cost is no longer the sole factor in evaluating the supply chain. Cost still plays a role, but it is a secondary role. The outcome becomes the primary object of the evaluation. In the past, measuring supply chain performance focused on production, be it patient days or discharges (with a concentration on the cost per). The supply chain tried to reduce cost at every turn, with less emphasis given to the quality of the production. By adding this new gauge, a new point of emphasis has been created between the clinical operation and the supply chain, with the understanding that changes in the supply chain may be necessary to create improvements in quality. The impact on supply expense per may be unknown under this methodology, but there should be a reduction in total cost per.

# IX

# Establishing a Physician-Led Value Analysis Process

CONTRIBUTORS

Jeffrey Ashkenase | Kristin Boehm, MD | Sandra Monacelli, RN

Historically, supply chain decisions haven't involved physicians or other clinicians beyond the products they request. However, in an era of fixed reimbursement, the type of products selected and the degree to which they are used can have significant financial repercussions. The ability of hospitals and health systems to use outcomes data and comparative effectiveness to make informed clinical decisions—from treatment protocols to device selection—is more important than ever. This requires a very different level of teamwork. Supply chain departments and clinical end users can no longer work independently of each other but instead need to meet in the middle, particularly when it comes to product decisions. Organizations that encourage their clinicians to be true stewards of healthcare resources, not just care providers, are the ones that are most likely to thrive.

Hospitals are increasingly turning to value analysis to foster collaboration between clinicians, supply chain personnel, executive leadership, and vendors. By breaking down longstanding institutional silos, relevant stakeholders are collaborating on an array of initiatives from conception to implementation and influencing decisions on the products being used. Best practice value analysis goes well beyond typical product selection. It nurtures a culture of shared accountability and is a means to improve quality, reduce operating expenses, and measure if the products being used are in fact delivering clinical results at a price that maximizes reimbursement. This form of value analysis fulfills every facet of CQO.

### Make value analysis a physician-led process
Physicians influence most product decisions, particularly those in the physician preference item space. Therefore, involving physicians in new product selection dramatically increases the likelihood of successful value analysis. Too often clinicians are faced with the results of one-sided decisions by individuals who lack a big picture view of products and the outcomes they deliver. While hospitals and systems can no longer afford to grant physicians indiscriminate buying authority, physicians remain integral to a successful value-based purchasing strategy.

A physician-led value analysis program consisting of teams that have representation from supply chain, finance, information technology, biomedical engineering, nursing, and other service lines creates a platform for developing strategic cost-reduction initiatives that support quality and safety measures, outstanding clinical outcomes, and decreased supply utilization across one or multiple facilities. In best practice physician-led value analysis, teams establish objective criteria for evidence-based evaluations—ensuring that key stakeholders are involved—and assign additional members when specialized knowledge or representation is needed. This level of objectivity brings evidence-based medicine and the tenets of clinical best practice to the discussion, and drives a process that improves quality and patient outcomes while reducing cost.

### Obtain C-suite support
Implementing physician-led value analysis requires cultural transformation. The traditional silos that are inherent in many provider settings must be broken down in order to create an environment in which supply chain, finance, information technology, infection control, and patient-facing professionals can work together. Operating at the intersection of CQO can be introduced as their objective, with value analysis as the collaborative method that can be used to achieve their goal.

Therefore, value analysis must be actively supported by executives who have the authority to drive cultural transformation, institute new processes, and hold everyone accountable. They can help ensure acceptance at all levels of the organization—and by all entities within an integrated delivery network. Support from these executives must be consistent and visible, and ideally it should demonstrate the importance of quality as well as cost when it comes to hospital decision-making in order to align the system's strategic vision with value analysis. This level of executive support involves ongoing dialogue; education about the value analysis process; alignment with clinicians, value analysis team members, and other stakeholders; and the C-suite's willingness to communicate their support of the supply chain manager's need to challenge the status quo and break down cost barriers.

To ensure this level of ongoing support, it is helpful to have a Value Analysis Executive Steering Committee (see Figure) that consists of C-suite, clinical, and administrative leadership. The Executive Steering Committee provides organizational direction, establishes goals, and assigns accountability for overall value analysis processes and deliverables. Most important, this type of hierarchy ensures that there is a platform for conflict resolution when inevitable barriers arise that need to be addressed with a certain level of authority.

FIGURE

## Sample Value Analysis Structure

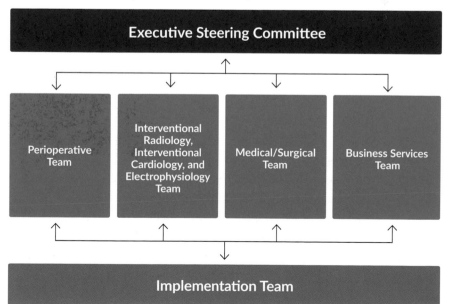

## Best Practice Value Analysis Elements

A best practice value analysis program includes the following elements:
- Executive support
- Accountability
- Transparency
- Consistency
- Standardization
- High reliability

### Create a value analysis structure

Value analysis must have a clearly defined process and governance structure in order to successfully achieve and sustain positive change.

*Build effective relationships with stakeholders*

A key piece of healthcare transformation is moving to a patient-centered, team-based approach to care delivery. Value analysis is the forum where individuals from the supply chain, finance, and other non-clinical areas can better understand the physicians' environment, and vice versa. Willingness and understanding can go a long way to building the trust and camaraderie that are the foundation of a strong, lasting partnership between physicians, clinicians, the supply chain, and administration. Supply chain professionals and value analysis directors must build trust with their clinical and subject matter stakeholders in order to develop credibility and secure participation. A good way to appeal to clinicians is through product fairs and clinical trials rather than by making immediate product changes. This may be new territory for some people, so educating them about each step of the process can be reassuring and often enlightening. Be attentive and responsive, invite their opinions, and secure physician champions.

*Formalize the process*

In time, value analysis should become the primary method for making new purchasing decisions. Value analysis teams must create a standardized process for how purchasing requests are added to a meeting schedule and decisions are made. This includes assessing existing products that have a contract that is ending or new products that may require a clear clinical or business case for being introduced. Each organization must create a process that works best for its needs and culture.

A sure way to doom a well-intentioned program is to leave meeting schedules and plans for next steps unassigned. Schedule regular meetings and provide team members with published agendas ahead of time. Don't allow ad hoc meetings. To maintain momentum, follow up on previous initiatives and action items before the next scheduled meeting occurs. Meetings that are canceled repeatedly or situations in which assigned tasks are not dealt with or are carried over from previous meetings convey a lack of importance and coordination that can easily derail motivation. Keep in mind that time is one of a physician's most valuable commodities. Value analysis activities need to yield timely, tangible results in order to maintain ongoing physician participation. Certain aspects can negatively impact perception and quickly discourage surgeons. This can include scheduling meetings at inopportune times, creating a cumbersome process, or taking an excessive amount of time to complete clinical initiatives. These will all but guarantee poor physician participation and will subsequently undermine the overall process. Create a meeting schedule that will ensure that the majority of the team is able to attend.

Each meeting should include a review of financial information, clinical information, customer satisfaction, and the impact of information technology. Suggestions for new product discussions can come from clinicians, vendors, and staff. The final decision regarding what will be discussed is made by the Executive Steering Committee.

Coordinating all aspects of successful value analysis and maintaining forward momentum is a full-time job. Having a dedicated value analysis director whose sole responsibility is to create an actionable, sustainable process increases the likelihood of it being effective and unburdens those in supply chain and nursing who have competing priorities and may lack the time to dedicate to the process.

*Track results and communicate success stories*
A key element of value analysis is understanding the impact of decisions and tracking results. Organizations need to ensure that they are seeing positive results or put in corrective action plans if things are not going as expected. Ideally, review reports monthly but no less than quarterly.

Build organization-wide support by communicating value analysis success stories. This creates a positive environment, builds consensus, and motivates others throughout the institution to embrace an agenda that supports CQO. For example, creative value analysis directors can not only send emails to the whole organization about product or process changes but also report the savings incurred and honor the key individuals involved in the change. Put up a scorecard in the OR lounge or physician lunchroom, postings in hospital newsletters, and report all team savings to a central steering group. While it is important to communicate the success of value analysis initiatives system-wide, it is equally important to communicate with the supply chain team. Consistent internal discussions keep initiatives moving, address barriers, and convey the value of the team.

Value analysis should become rooted in everyday operations and be a part of the organizational purchasing mindset. Before any new product is purchased, the value analysis team should be the first stop. The expectation organization-wide should be that any request needs to be supported with a well-articulated value proposition. Value analysis is the impetus for the change management necessary for meeting value-based goals and operating at the intersection of CQO.

## Building Critical Supply Chain Skill Sets

A well-performing, collaborative supply chain must be in place when initiating a physician-led process. If not, the process will be out of sync and result in decreased engagement and stalled productivity. By implementing a physician-led process backed by the support of a dedicated value analysis director, the supply chain team will learn how to carry out value analysis initiatives by doing the following:

- Understanding the economics of a product or service beyond its price
- Partnering with the C-suite as needed
- Implementing initiatives
- Building and maintaining relationships with clinicians
- Managing more than just the cost of items
- Collaborating with stakeholders across the continuum of care

BEST PRACTICE

**Engage clinicians with the right data**

Just as clinician engagement is critical to successful value analysis, data is critical to engaging clinicians. When discussing purchasing patterns with clinicians, be equipped with relevant data. In an environment where physicians are being asked to present evidence-based medicine to support their product decisions, it is equally important for supply chain to access and present the cost analytics and benchmarks that support strategic purchasing decisions in an organized fashion.

The new metrics outlined in the previous chapter—which focus on tying supply purchases to clinical conditions and outcomes—are a perfect example of the type of data required to engage physicians and other clinicians in functionally equivalent product discussions and the prudent use of hospital resources.

The supply chain should be prepared to bring both qualitative and quantitative information to value analysis discussions, such as the following:

- Spend data
- Quality/outcomes data
- Revenue data
- Resource use
- Benchmarks
- Regulatory changes

- Environment of care information
- Safety and prevention information
- Clinically/functionally equivalent product information

**KEY PERFORMANCE INDICATORS**

**The following can be used to measure supply chain performance in value analysis:**

- Annual savings ($)
  - Annual savings based on value analysis initiatives
- Value analysis initiative volume (%)
  - Value analysis initiatives ÷ total procurement initiatives

Case Study

# St. Luke's Cornwall Hospital

**About St. Luke's Cornwall Hospital**

St. Luke's Cornwall Hospital (SLCH) is an urban nonprofit hospital serving the Hudson Valley in New York State. With 272 beds, it is an outpatient-focused, critical care facility with a Level III Trauma Center. SLCH became an integrated delivery network in 2002. In 2016, it partnered with Montefiore Health System, making it part of a leading organization in population health management. SLCH serves over 270,000 patients annually, has 1,500 employees, and retains over 300 staff physicians representing dozens of medical specialties.

**Background**

In the past, the purchasing strategy at SLCH primarily focused on product evaluations that were based on cost instead of being centered on more strategic, evidence-based justifications. This approach to product requests and acquisition resulted in the following:

- The purchase of items that were often underused, due to a lack of complete physician buy-in or scenarios in which the requesting physician had left the organization
- Products that were only used until the next best item came to market (which typically occurred before any ROI was achieved)
- Items that were bought without supplementary stakeholder engagement, which led to problematic downstream issues, such as a lack of the electrical requirements at the point of service, lack of central sterile resources for maintenance, or lack of physical space

It was clear that the current structure was not sustainable, especially in a value-based environment. It was time for the organization to evolve.

**Methodology**

SLCH employed a mix of the right people, the right structure, and the right data to evaluate product requests through a newly established value analysis program. SLCH's executive leadership recognized that value analysis was a means to reduce costs without compromising care quality or outcomes. They built a value analysis program based on partnerships between clinical and administrative staffs, enabling multidisciplinary teams to facilitate collaborative saving opportunities. The teams use evidence-based clinical outcomes data to ensure that all product selection decisions optimize cost, quality, and patient outcomes.

The right data (which is primarily the responsibility of the supply chain analyst and data integrity manager) includes PO history, the item master list, general ledger spend, distribution partner order history, contracts loaded in the connectivity report, GPO contract list and activation status, and GPO contract opportunities. The vendor and GPO partners maintain secondary responsibility for this information.

The right structure includes an Executive Steering Committee and three value analysis teams: perioperative, medical/surgical and interventional, and business services. SLCH also established an implementation team. The duties of the implementation team are to coordinate the purchasing, receiving, and distribution of the value analysis-approved products or services while ensuring that old products are not wasted.

In terms of the right people, the Executive Steering Committee is chaired by a physician (the associate chief medical officer) who was appointed by the chief financial officer. The Executive Steering Committee chair selected the physician chairs for both the perioperative and medical/surgical and interventional teams, a decision that was based on the individuals' ability to engage other physicians and solicit feedback from their peers. The associate chief medical officer also sought physicians who were open to new opportunities, were perceived as influential, and were highly respected throughout the system. The physician chairs had to be invested in the success of value analysis outcomes.

The assistant vice president of revenue cycle and compliance chairs the business services team. Additional team members were selected by each committee chair with the help of the value analysis director. They include physicians, clinicians, members of the C-suite, and individuals from quality, infection control, nursing education, supply chain, and reimbursement.

To garner organization-wide support and to communicate the high priority of this effort, the chief financial officer and chief medical officer made introductory presentations at medical staff meetings in which the concept, process, and value analysis program rollout were communicated. Additional presentations were also given to various key stakeholders, such as nursing, infection control, and orthopedics. Further, the SLCH marketing department distributed introductory announcements via email to the entire hospital as well as issued an external press release.

Value analysis meetings are now held monthly and scheduled a year in advance. Meeting times are selected by each individual group. For example, the perioperative value analysis meeting is held at 6:30 a.m. to accommodate surgeons' hours and OR scheduling times, and the medical/surgical and interventional meeting is held in the late afternoon to accommodate the nursing staff and physicians who have office hours outside of the hospital.

Anything that touches supply chain and patient care is discussed at meetings. The agenda follows the same outline each meeting, including a review of initiatives that have either been approved or denied and are to be elevated to the Executive Steering Committee meeting. Initiatives that are in review are discussed and updated. New initiatives—whether a cost-saving opportunity, quality improvement campaign, or best practice suggestion— are presented to the committee for decision on whether or not to pursue. New product requests from physicians or staff are also presented at this time. The last item on the agenda is a discussion that can be used to communicate additional information to team members (e.g., recalls, backorders) and other proposed review topics.

The value analysis director is responsible for following up with physicians, the chair of the Executive Steering Committee, and the chief financial officer as needed. In an effort to make additional interactions most convenient for physicians, these meetings are typically held in doctors' offices or clinical settings and occur early in the morning before cases begin or in the evenings when the work day has concluded.

## Results

Since implementing value analysis at SLCH, the impact has been felt throughout the hospital. There has been a culture shift geared to process transparency and standardization (driven by C-suite and physician support). There is now an expectation that product requests need to be supported with specific, articulated value-adds, where value takes CQO into account and is supported with clinical-based evidence. There is even friendly competition among the teams as initiatives are categorized by team with totals listed and tallied. Each team strives to attain the most savings and value. In the first three years of the value analysis program, SLCH saved $4.25 million while positively impacting quality and outcomes.

# Value Analysis in Action

*Three examples of the impact of physician-led*
*value analysis on improved outcomes*

PRODUCT 1
**Peripheral intervenous (IV) catheter**

PROVIDER 1
**500+ bed medical center**

## Background

The medical center's current IV catheter routinely leaked blood from the catheter hub immediately upon insertion, exposing caregivers to potential blood-borne hazards. The issue was brought to the medical/surgical value analysis team, with the goal of improving clinician safety related to potential exposure to blood-borne pathogens at the IV insertion site. Finding an alternative product that didn't pose the same degree of risk was a priority.

Simultaneously, blood-borne contamination of the IV insertion site was leading to increased supply and personnel costs, creating a financial imperative for change.

## Methodology

The value analysis team evaluated alternative products, finding one that offered the most benefits, including the following:

- Increased clinician safety, due to blood control technology/reduced blood exposure
- Proprietary vialon catheter material extending the dwell time of the IV catheter, reducing catheter complications and associated costs
- Reduced blood cleanup, helping to reduce supply costs and improve nursing efficiency, due to reduced cleanup time
- Technology designed to improve first stick proficiency and minimize painful missed insertions

## Results

- A 5% annual cost savings
- Supply and personnel costs associated with blood-borne contamination of the IV insertion site significantly reduced or eliminated through the use of this product
- Quality significantly improved based on the elimination of blood leakage at the IV insertion site
- Improved financial and clinical outcomes through patient and employee satisfaction

PRODUCT 2 — **Contrast media**

PROVIDER 2 — **Integrated delivery network**

## Background

The nurse manager of interventional radiology, the electrophysiology lab, and the cath lab noticed that contrast media use was way over budget. He contacted the interventional value analysis team for help. The data team found that Iodixanol (Visipaque®) use was rising at a rapid rate, and Iohexal (Omnipaque®) use was declining to almost nothing (Visipaque and Omnipaque are dyes).

## Methodology

Through interventional value analysis team discussions, it was determined that nursing staff were using Visipaque for almost all cases, as they did not want to change the power injector to use Omnipaque. Visipaque is three times as expensive as Omnipaque. Following research, it was agreed by the physicians (including the radiologist and interventional cardiologist champions) that Omnipaque could and should be used for most cases, with few exceptions. The value analysis team—in collaboration with radiologists and physicians—created a policy and procedure for contrast media use, educated the nursing and physician staff, and are holding them accountable.

## Results

- Savings on use alone was $279,515, improving financial outcomes
- A request for proposal for price reduction secured an additional $132,917 in savings

PRODUCT 3                    PROVIDER 3
**Venous access devices**     **300+ bed urban community hospital**

### Background

The hospital was seeing high rates of CLABSI, resulting in adverse patient events, extended patient stays, and increased cost of care and reduced reimbursement. They reported 24 CLABSI cases in a 12-month period at an average cost of $45,000 per infection. The hospital used multiple vendors and products for venous access devices; however, all were non-impregnated (regular) catheters. This resulted in increased supply chain costs, low-quality processes, and poor financial outcomes.

### Methodology

The physician-led value analysis team recommended a change to a high-quality product with chlorhexidine-impregnated catheters (catheters saturated in antimicrobial substance) to reduce patient risk of CLABSI. The hospital standardized purchasing to a single manufacturer, a high-value product with antimicrobial catheters, and developed a calculation methodology to monitor the results. A mutual agreement between the hospital and the selected vendor was made to assess current practices, educate clinicians on best practice, and re-evaluate quarterly to measure the impact.

### Results

The value analysis team worked with the hospital's infection prevention department to track occurrences of CLABSI. Simultaneously, the value analysis team facilitated vendor-provided education on best practice catheter placement and care. The value analysis team provides a quarterly lookback to continually monitor results. The improvements included the following:

- A 50% reduction in CLABSI infection rates
- Reduction in hospital-acquired condition penalties
- Total infection prevention savings: $550,351

## X.

# Creating an Outcomes-Based Contracting Strategy

**CONTRIBUTORS**

Robert Karcher | Praful Shah

Contracting is the process in which a provider signs an agreement with a vendor for a service or an item at a particular price, usually for a fixed time period. While pricing for food, fuel, and other commodities may vary as often as daily, purchasing items from fixed-price contracts helps hospitals better anticipate costs (and budgets) by ensuring that the pricing terms negotiated with approved vendors are stable over the course of the agreement. Contracts also provide conditions of product quality and warranties—among other conditions—that both parties agree to over the life of the purchasing agreement. Value-added discounts and rebates that the purchaser receives if certain conditions are met as well as potential vendor penalties for failure to provide goods or services, or for failure to meet the delivery, quality, or availability requirements outlined in the terms and conditions, may also be included in a contract. In light of real-world incidents, any cybersecurity-related concerns should also be addressed in a contract.

Using comprehensive, efficient contract management for all regularly purchased stock products and services is important to providing quality care at an affordable cost. While price is always a critical factor (and the basic reason for a contract), a product's ability to affect patient outcomes positively—such as shortening the length of stay, reducing or eliminating the likelihood of hospital-acquired conditions, or minimizing the potential of a post-discharge illness that necessitates readmission—is an important consideration. While these clinical benefits are worth considering in and of themselves, providers must factor the financial implications of such outcomes into the total delivered cost of an episode of care.

An organization operating at the intersection of CQO uses value analysis to determine which item to purchase based on evidence that demonstrates that item's impact on the clinical and financial outcomes of the procedure for which it is used. The organization then uses an outcomes-based contracting approach to create an implicit relationship between the hospital and the product vendor to manage patient care jointly.

Outcomes-based contracting looks at the total cost of a product (from sourcing to reimbursement) and requires that the vendor play a role in supporting the provider's transition to value-based reimbursement by agreeing to share either savings or risk based on the ability of its product to improve patient outcomes. In this sense, outcomes-based contracting is by definition risk-based contracting.

Both hospitals and vendors have reason to align: hospitals want to treat patients successfully in a financially viable manner; vendors wants to grow business with hospitals. Vendors are eager to provide value beyond price, assuming there is a good match between their product and a significantly beneficial outcome. Put a different way, as hospitals are reimbursed based on outcomes, they look to work with vendors with whom they can ensure those outcomes and share risk.

There are, however, many barriers to overcome when introducing a progressive outcomes-based contracting approach, such as an entrenched culture, offering transparency to an outside party (the vendor), dependence on effective data reporting, collaboration between clinicians and non-clinicians making an investment in quality, and developing new contract language. Outcomes-based contracting necessitates a significant culture change and requires accurate quality and outcome reporting—which is still evolving. However, when conducted properly, this kind of agreement can provide long-term quality and financial benefits to an organization.

As this is a much more time- and labor-intensive approach than traditional bid-and-award sourcing, it should be reserved for specific products that promise significantly improved outcomes and not be used for routine purchases. Medical devices, for example, are particularly relevant to this approach. The traditional method of looking at total delivered cost is usually applied to capital equipment, such as intravenous pumps, with long-term amortization, maintenance, and utilization schedules. However, the supply chain must begin to apply a total delivered cost approach to other items (such as single-use medical devices) in order to understand the effect these items have on patient outcomes and build a risk/reward relationship with vendors. This advanced approach represents the culmination of the supply chain's transformation from transactional to strategic. To conduct outcomes-based contracting, supply chain professionals must be prepared to do the following:

- Identify all components of an item or procedure that might impact outcomes
- Identify internal quality reporting metrics (e.g., length of stay, infection rates) that would help demonstrate that an item is improving care or meeting a predetermined outcome
- Isolate the outcome in a way that demonstrates that the product change was the cause (or contributed to the cause)
- Negotiate with vendors and hospital leadership to accept this model
  - As part of this discussion, receive authorization from both internal and vendor leadership that they will be held accountable for changes in the predetermined outcome and the subsequent risk payments or shared rewards
- Confirm that the agreed-upon metric determines the outcome
- Apply the rate of performance to the risk/reward benefit in a way that can demonstrate the product is responsible for the benefit
- Periodically measure outcomes and compare them to baseline to ensure that benefits continue to be demonstrated
- Ensure that this reporting can be replicated

## Outcomes-Based Contracting in Practice

Silver-coated urinary (Foley) catheter manufacturers provided an early (mid-1990s) example of outcomes-based contracting. Because of the antimicrobial properties of silver, it can potentially reduce the rate of urinary tract and bloodstream infections. These hospital-acquired infections have a financial impact. They require expensive inpatient care over a longer time, the use of antibiotics, and they can potentially result in litigation.

*(continued on next page)*

> ## Outcomes-Based Contracting in Practice
> *(continued)*
>
> But adding a precious metal to a urinary catheter raises its price significantly.
>
> The coated catheter vendors paid for studies that quantified the cost per incident of these negative outcomes. To encourage hospitals to invest in the new, far more expensive catheters, vendors allowed hospitals to purchase the silver-coated catheters at the then-current price of uncoated catheters for a period of time if the hospital would share its baseline infection rate statistics with them. If the number of urinary or bloodstream infections decreased over the agreed trial period—therefore lowering the total cost of care for catheterized patients—the hospital would begin to pay the higher price for the silver-coated catheters. This is an example of a supplier investing in quality that results in a shared reward.

### BEST PRACTICE
**Improve fundamental operations before exploring outcomes-based methods**
The supply chain's contracting process must be buttoned up before it can take on more strategic endeavors. To this end, hospitals should first assess current supply chain contracting performance before considering outcomes-based opportunities. The following parameters are good indicators of a supply chain's readiness:

- At least 75% of the hospital's predictable purchase expenses are on fixed-price contracts
- Contracts are centralized in a single electronic requisitioning program across the enterprise (individual departments should not be contracting independently)
- Hospital maintains a database of prices and usage that can be reported by specific end user (cost center)
- The hospital's GPO is used for a majority of its product purchases
- Contract pricing is regularly validated to ensure that the provider is getting the agreed-upon price
- Hospital collects and maintains all state and federally required quality metrics

- Contracts are electronically activated, validated, and maintained
- There is a mandate to ensure that those contracts in GPO categories that must be negotiated locally are executed using GPO-vendor reporting
- Value-added services—such as analytics support—from the hospital's primary GPO are used broadly

Culture and governance are also critical to outcomes-based contracting. Leadership should assess if the hospital environment is suitable for this progressive approach. The following steps should be taken to ready your organization:

- Starting with the chief executive officer and the C-suite, create a corporate culture that is dedicated to continuous improvement (see "The Fundamentals" chapter). Underscore the importance of multidisciplinary collaboration to achieve improved healthcare quality and outcomes; focus on processes, not people, when an adverse event occurs.
- Instill a team approach to purchasing that incorporates the C-suite, engaged clinicians (physicians, nurses, pharmacists), reimbursement managers, risk/quality managers, and clinical data managers. Like value analysis, outcomes-based contracting should involve all stakeholders and subject matter experts who can provide insight into metrics and other factors.
- Because outcomes-based contracting is a longer, more complicated process, key stakeholders should determine which product groups to target and then assign an individual to report on the short- and long-term results. In traditional contracting, purchasing decisions are the purview of the supply chain because price is the main factor. But with so many departments involved in outcomes-based contracting, it can be hard to determine who owns the process. The chief financial officer or the chief risk/quality officer may be in the best position to take on this role, as there may be hospital-wide implications.
- Work with the chief financial officer or the individual who is responsible for the initiative to help them understand the long-term benefit of this new approach and to ensure that the right resources are dedicated to it.

BEST PRACTICE
## Establish a test model

Implementing outcomes-based contracting is best accomplished using several easily quantifiable achievements to build momentum toward a full value-based approach. Start small, with one product and one measurement, both of which pertain to one clinical outcome. The team can begin by identifying a single product—perhaps a device that supports a procedure that is expected to generate a good outcome and margin or a product that has a track record of positive clinical outcomes.

Not all products are appropriate. The best products and services are specific enough to determine a particular outcome. For example, a good choice might be an implantable pressure sensor that can remotely signal the onset of congestive heart failure. The implant—which is inserted into the pulmonary artery and sends a radio frequency signal to the physician that a patient is going into congestive heart failure—provides an opportunity for the hospital to intervene (prescribe a change in diet, medication, etc.) before a readmission becomes necessary. Since readmissions within 30 days of discharge for the same diagnosis are not reimbursed, there is a clear cost avoidance for monitoring patients in a congestive heart failure program. This can include measuring readmissions without the sensor against those who receive the sensor. While an implantable pressure sensor is expensive, it is significantly less expensive than the cost of care for a full readmission with no reimbursement.

Chosen carefully, some medical products can help shorten lengths of stay, minimize readmissions, and avoid a never event. These positive outcomes not only benefit the patient, they also help hospitals avoid unnecessary costs or they increase the contribution margin (amount of reimbursement the hospital receives above the cost of care) associated with an inpatient procedure or hospital stay.

It is important to ask the following questions before considering an outcomes-based contract engagement:

- Does the product have the potential to improve an outcome, prevent a longer hospital stay, avoid a readmission, enable a treatment to be administered or a procedure to be performed on an outpatient basis, or avoid a common inpatient pitfall or adverse event?

- If so, can any of the benefits, penalties, or increased costs associated with these outcomes be quantified through in-house verifiable reporting?
- Does the clinical "owner" or risk manager in the hospital agree that there is a definite correlation between the product and the beneficial outcome?

Once the contracting team has determined the acquisition strategy and risk versus reward, it's time to approach the vendor.

BEST PRACTICE

**Change the conversation to improve the provider-vendor relationship**

The supply chain-vendor relationship can be contentious. Vendors hold out for the highest price, while supply chain executives try to drive as much margin out of the transaction as possible. Entering into a risk-based purchasing relationship requires a change in this dynamic. Both parties must be transparent about their expectations and willing to commit to making good on the outcome, whether it's the hospital sharing a benefit with a vendor or the vendor sharing the cost of an adverse outcome. While almost every vendor will publically market its product as the very best for patient care, it becomes a more serious matter when they stake their profit margin on it. Just because vendors like to push bottom-line cost to the periphery of the negotiation, it doesn't necessarily mean they are prepared to live with (or sell to their management) a transaction based on risk that has the potential for zero profit, or worse, a loss.

The hospital supply chain must be able to convince its financial and clinical leadership that the risk of increased cost, potentially without a demonstrable improved outcome, is a risk worth taking. A contracting team will likely be skeptical about a vendor's product assertions. This is where trusted subject matter experts can be brought in to validate vendor claims of efficacy. When it comes to evaluating an item before engaging a vendor, clinical peers are ideal. For example, if a hospital is considering an outcomes-based contract for equipment that reinfuses a patient's own blood perioperatively—thus reducing the hospital's dependence on expensive third-party transfusions—the supply chain executive should meet with surgeons and perfusionists who have experience and positive outcomes using cell saver equipment during cardiac, orthopedic, or other blood-dependent surgeries.

To make outcomes-based contracting work, both parties must invest in the relationship. Providers must be willing to take a leap of faith, and vendors must be willing to have skin in the game.

BEST PRACTICE
## Involve a GPO

A new paradigm for many supply chain professionals—involving the hospital's GPO—can help kick-start discussions, build confidence, and potentially bring both parties to the table. The GPO often has the resources (time, analytics, access to data, references) to identify viable product choices for an outcomes-based arrangement as well as the capacity to perform due diligence and test risk-based models with national representatives from the vendor community. A GPO may also know if there is already a working model in another part of the country.

Because GPOs are advocates for their members, a hospital is more likely to trust its relationship with its GPO than with a vendor. That relationship can be leveraged to support value-based contracting initiatives. The GPO's purchasing and analytics experts can provide direction for narrowing down product choices, provide examples of successful risk-based contracting models, and bridge the gap between the provider and the vendor to initiate value-based negotiations.

GPOs can also help hospitals develop the value analysis infrastructure necessary to connect the supply chain with clinical leadership and risk managers so that they can properly assess and validate the right approach for the hospital. Enlisting a multidisciplinary team within the institution is critical to the success of outcomes-based contracting.

BEST PRACTICE
## Select metrics to negotiate the contract carefully

Risk-sharing or shared-savings agreements between a hospital and a vendor rely on data (accurate data is essential for measuring whether an item is meeting the performance goal). As state and federal regulations and reimbursement methods continue to generate more outcomes-based reporting, the metrics necessary for outcomes-based contracts become more widely available. See the "Capturing and Applying Alternative Data Sets" chapter for more information about the alternative data sets required for these types of agreements.

Hospitals and vendors must carefully negotiate a shared-savings or risk-sharing agreement that includes descriptions of the following:

- The metric that will be used to measure performance
- The quantifiable cost of that outcome or penalty avoidance
- A mutually agreed-upon baseline
- The time period that will influence a change in the baseline
- An acceptable performance goal
- An agreed-upon reporting mechanism
- The penalty or benefit that the vendor will incur based on performance
    - Will the vendor share the savings?
    - Will the vendor pay a penalty?
    - Will the vendor accept the result?

Developing this kind of contract also means sharing data (good or bad) with the vendor. This is another new concept for hospitals, and it represents a change in culture. Sharing data becomes more palatable if the outcome is already publically reported. All outcomes reporting must be patient-blinded and free of any HIPAA privacy violations.

**KEY PERFORMANCE INDICATORS**

**The following can be used to measure supply chain performance in contracting:**

- On-contract PO spend (%)
- Supply spend as a percentage of net operating revenue (%)
    - Supply spend ÷ net operating revenue

Case Study

# Mount Sinai Health System

### About Mount Sinai Health System

Mount Sinai Health System (Mount Sinai) is composed of seven hospital campuses, the Icahn School of Medicine at Mount Sinai, nine operating ambulatory care centers, two urgent care joint ventures, and 300 community locations throughout the New York City metropolitan area. There are 138 ORs and 3,468 beds. The entire health system employs more than 38,000 people, including more than 6,500 physicians, and more than 2,000 residents and clinical fellows.

### Background

In 2013, Mount Sinai and Continuum Health Partners merged, bringing additional acute care hospitals and other facilities into the Mount Sinai Health System. Hospitals across the newly merged system had different cultures, workflows, approval paths, and standard operating procedures. The hospitals had their own item masters and contract repositories, different value analysis team models, and were doing business on four different MMIS platforms. The average combined contract spend was under 75%.

Mount Sinai's leadership had several goals. They wanted to centralize contracting decisions and product evaluations, create a robust value analysis structure, consolidate vendor contracts for specific products and service categories, and keep all contracts in a single repository to help leverage the system's size and spend to get even more competitive pricing and achieve additional cost savings.

## Methodology

The Mount Sinai supply chain team used an existing clinical data warehouse to support the new structure and contracting initiatives by consolidating the purchasing transactions from its four MMISs into a space designed for supply chain's exclusive use. This new centralized repository first identified price parity issues and is now used to identify new contracting opportunities. Communication between the sourcing department, clinicians, and end users was also improved as a result of the accuracy and accessibility of this consolidated information. Supply chain has been able to generate reports and gather information much more efficiently from this single data source, which has proved invaluable for aligning spend, transactions, and contracting.

Mount Sinai also focused on entering into contracts using CQO principles. To do this, they used sourcing negotiation and clinician input and created value analysis committees through which products/services were more stringently evaluated. In many cases, products were deemed worthy of consideration for CQO-based agreements, such as shared risk tied to patient outcomes. The value analysis teams are organized by product category (such as medical/surgical, business, and cardiology/interventional radiology). Each team has a hospital leadership champion; clinical committees are chaired by physicians and clinicians.

## Results

Mount Sinai now has three item masters, which are all combined into a virtual item master. Local contracts are also housed in the system along with GPO pricing agreements. Coupled with the data warehouse, these solutions have been used to facilitate the data and pricing aggregation work used to create and renegotiate contracts.

Contracts are examined to see how they will contribute to attaining CQO. Mount Sinai has also hired a data science analyst who works with clinicians and provides analytical support on all value analysis initiatives as well as a true cost total joint initiative. Contract negotiations are centralized and include physicians, clinicians, sourcing, and materials management. Mount Sinai has also created risk-sharing agreements to reduce the incidence of CLABSI.

There are now clinically driven value analysis teams in which all stakeholders are represented, and the value analysis contracting initiatives have been projected and completed in a timely, efficient manner. The system has a pipeline of value analysis projects that includes anticipated savings and implementation dates to help keep committees on track.

By building a new value analysis structure and centralizing its contracting, Mount Sinai achieved more than $100 million in savings between 2014 and 2016, and increased its contract spend to 85%.

# The University of Tennessee Medical Center

**About The University of Tennessee Medical Center**

The University of Tennessee Medical Center (UT Medical Center) is a 599-bed academic medical center located in Knoxville. It serves as the major referral center for Eastern Tennessee, Southern Kentucky, and Western North Carolina. The Emergency and Trauma Center, one of six centers of excellence at UT Medical Center, is the region's Level I Trauma Center and tertiary referral center for the one million adults and children living in the tristate region. The other five centers of excellence—the Advanced Orthopaedic Center, Women & Infants Center, Cancer Institute, Brain & Spine Institute, and the Heart Lung Vascular Institute—provide a high level of care to patients in need.

**Background**

The UT Medical Center Heart Lung Vascular Institute faced recurring platelet shortages, which were especially acute early in the week. Cardio-thoracic surgeons who scheduled procedures to begin promptly every Monday would too often have to delay or reschedule procedures when the hospital blood bank was unable to procure sufficient platelets to meet their needs.

The Emergency and Trauma Center faced a similar issue in dealing with a critical, recurring shortage of type O negative blood. Trauma centers require a ready stock of type O negative blood to treat patients of unknown blood type who require emergency transfusions.

Simultaneously, the hospital was pursuing a system-wide cost-reduction initiative. The hospital critically needed to use a service to supplement its current blood procurement efforts without overpaying. They identified cost of services and timely execution of scheduled procedures as vital components of the initiative. There could be no compromise on patient outcomes, however, even with the pressure to lower costs.

UT Medical Center had a decades-long partnership with their local blood center. But the hospital's growth and the population it served had outstripped the blood center's ability to meet the needs of UT Medical Center, significantly straining the partnership. The strain was complicating the blood bank's ability to help the cost and clinical improvement initiative getting underway at UT Medical Center.

## Methodology

UT Medical Center decided to use a distributed supply network and adopt new (but proven) technological innovations, an approach that was in line with recommendations in the 2016 RAND Corporation report, "Toward a Sustainable Blood Supply in the United States," commissioned by the National Institutes of Health. To mitigate shortages and costs, UT Medical Center entered into a relationship with Bloodbuy®. Bloodbuy provides direct access to a diversified network of industry-leading blood centers, ensuring that they have the blood products they need, when they need them, without overpaying.

Key UT Medical Center stakeholders worked collaboratively with the Bloodbuy team to identify critical inventory challenges. With access to the Bloodbuy platform, UT Medical Center established recurring platelet orders throughout the week to ensure a sufficient buffer for scheduled cardiothoracic surgeries. The standing orders established and managed via the Bloodbuy platform eliminated the platelet inventory issues.

Bloodbuy was able to connect UT Medical Center with blood centers that enhanced their overall supply of red cells for all blood types, including the crucial type O negative red blood cells, which are in high demand nationwide because of the essential role they play in emergency situations.

The Bloodbuy platform was specifically built to maintain cost awareness—an essential component for meeting UT Medical Center's goals. Before procuring units, UT Medical Center fully evaluated the projected expense for each order. Due to regional imbalances in production costs and oversupply of units at some blood centers, UT Medical Center met their needs with significant savings relative to existing price per unit.

Until recently, all platelet products produced by American blood centers were single-donor platelets (SDPs). SDP donors are difficult to recruit and highly valued. Bloodbuy connected UT Medical Center with a blood center licensed to produce Acrodose™ units (a method that allows blood centers to manufacture a unit of platelets by pooling platelets from four to five whole blood cell donations). Acrodose units cost less to produce than SDPs and use a fraction of a whole blood donation that is commonly discarded during production. This enabled UT Medical Center to augment their access to much-needed platelet products at a greatly reduced per unit cost.

## Results

Since partnering with Bloodbuy, no UT Medical Center patients have been negatively impacted due to a lack of blood product. UT Medical Center has had a 100% fill rate on orders placed through Bloodbuy while realizing an average 20% cost savings. The impact on patient outcomes has been significant. Since the Bloodbuy partnership, no cardiothoracic procedures have been rescheduled because of platelet shortages. Likewise, the blood bank has supplied their Emergency and Trauma Center with type O negative red blood cells in times of critical need.

The 20% cost savings realized via the Bloodbuy platform has resulted in a net savings of $60,000 over the 10 months UT Medical Center has used Bloodbuy as a secondary source of blood products. Beyond simple cost-per-unit, the increased product availability has allowed UT Medical Center's surgical units to operate closer to capacity, with less downtime and fewer patient disruptions. In 2016, UT Medical Center was the only facility in Tennessee to receive the highest rating of excellence from the Baldridge Performance Excellence Program, a National Institute of Standards and Technology project focused on operational excellence in large orgnizations.

By connecting with a national Bloodbuy platform network, UT Medical Center reduced pressure on their local blood center. The additional supply of type O negative red blood cells freed up local supplies, the hospital blood bank was sufficiently stocked to handle multiple emergencies, and the blood center retained a strategic reserve to serve a larger geographic area on an as-needed basis.

As an added benefit, since the local blood center did not produce Acrodose units, by accessing an entirely novel category of blood product, net pressure on local platelet production was relieved.

Finally, the entry of Bloodbuy as a trusted supplier for UT Medical Center has resulted in a stronger relationship between the hospital and their local blood center. As UT Medical Center accessed products that were not available locally, the blood center was able to focus on their core competencies. Competition has also resulted in an enhanced service level between UT Medical Center and their local blood products supplier. Ultimately, by working with more suppliers, UT Medical Center has increased the net amount of lifesaving blood products available to a regional population of over one million adults and children.

*Disclaimer: Bloodbuy is owned, in part, by Premier Supply Chain Improvement, Inc., an affiliate of Premier, Inc. ("Premier"). In addition, Premier and/or its affiliates have other contractual relationships with Bloodbuy, pursuant to which Premier may receive remuneration based on purchases of Bloodbuy's products or services by members of Acurity's or Premier's group purchasing program. An affiliate of Acurity is a partial owner of Premier and/or its affiliates.*

# Next Steps

---

# XI

# Achieving Optimal Supply Chain Performance: A Summary of Best Practices

I n the past, supply chain professionals have had to balance the need to reduce supply costs with the responsibility of meeting the needs of clinicians. In the world of value-based care, the responsibility for lowering total costs while improving care quality and outcomes is shared organization-wide. Everyone in a healthcare institution must be accountable for their role in operating at the intersection of CQO. This places supply chain professionals in an excellent position to use their experience and unique skill set to lead CQO-based discussions and contribute strategic, forward-thinking solutions that better their organization's financial status while improving patient care. Supply chain professionals are no longer transactional order takers, but rather individuals with a valuable opportunity to positively impact patients' lives. The time has come for the healthcare supply chain to secure a seat at the decision-making table.

Each chapter in this book includes best practices for achieving optimal performance in the central areas of supply chain operations as well as additional areas that are closely tied to the supply chain in a value-based environment. Here is a summary of those best practices organized by focus area.

**The Fundamentals**
- Establish internal controls for the supply chain
- Promote continuous process improvement
- Provide staff education

**Data Management**
- Create and maintain a clean, robust item master
- Standardize data using unique identifiers
- Build interfaces between the hospital's systems

**Requisitioning**
- Have a standardized requisition process to eliminate rogue spending
- Establish approval pathways for off-contract supplies

**Purchasing**
- Verify contract coverage for product requests
- Gather as much information as possible before processing orders
- Use data management to make purchasing more strategic
- Support internal customers

**Receiving**
- Make the best use of the space available
- Establish a synergistic delivery schedule
- Have a standard procedure for validating items
- Use strategic inventory management and distribution methods
- Establish policies and procedures for special types of inbound and outbound freight

**Distribution**
- Foster a culture of constant customer service
- Employ Lean principles in the predistribution area and delivery planning
- Develop delivery schedules and work assignments based on data
- Create a system based on the distribution model

## Inventory Management
- Have an inventory control strategy
- Examine inventory cycle for constraints
- Use cycle counts to track inventory in unit-specific locations
- Rotate stock to avoid expiration and waste

## Finance and Reimbursement Metrics
- Familiarize the supply chain with a new suite of metrics
- Monitor the quality of new product alternatives
- Evaluate performance and create dashboards

## Value Analysis
- Make value analysis a physician-led process
- Obtain C-suite support
- Create a value analysis structure
- Engage clinicians with the right data

## Contracting (Outcomes-Based)
- Improve fundamental operations before exploring outcomes-based methods
- Establish an outcomes-based contracting test model
- Change the conversation to improve the provider-vendor relationship
- Involve a GPO
- Select metrics to negotiate the contract carefully

## XII.

# Measuring Your Performance: The Hospital Supply Chain Performance Self-Assessment

This book has explored how the hospital and health system supply chain can make incremental improvements in order to achieve optimal performance in the areas that most directly contribute to their organization's ability to operate at the intersection of CQO. Reading this book is the first step toward improving performance by better understanding what constitutes best practice for supply chain operations in a patient-centered healthcare environment. The next step in the pursuit of CQO is for hospital leaders and supply chain executives to consider where their supply chain department stands.

The Hospital Supply Chain Performance Self-Assessment™ is a free online tool created by Nexera's subject matter experts. This tool enables hospital and health system leaders to benchmark current supply chain performance against the areas covered in this book. In the assessment, each area consists of one or more attributes, and each attribute is defined by specific measures that reflect successive levels of performance. Recognizing that not all areas have the same impact on CQO, relative weights have been calculated for each individual area. These weights are applied when computing a hospital's overall composite score. Because there is no limit to the number of times the assessment can be taken, the tool is useful for monitoring progress in areas of weakness and ensuring that performance in areas of strength is maintained.

To take the Hospital Supply Chain Performance Self-Assessment, visit nexerainc.com/CQOAssessment. You will be asked to complete a brief form and upon clicking Submit, you will immediately be directed to the assessment. Respondents get their results upon completion and can share the survey with others in their organization to aggregate results for a bigger, more accurate overview of performance. We encourage readers to return to this book after getting their assessment results. The chapters that correspond to the areas identified by the assessment as those with the greatest need for improvement can serve as a guide for directing supply chain leaders on where to start.

We hope you have enjoyed this book. Supply chain management, its impact on CQO, and its potential effect on value-based care and population health will continue to evolve. We look forward to continuing to share our knowledge and offering you the resources to support your organization's pursuit of CQO.

# Acronyms and Abbreviations

ACA: Affordable Care Act

AHRMM: Association for Healthcare Resource & Materials Management

ANSI: American National Standards Institute

CAUTI: catheter-associated urinary tract infection

CDM code: chargemaster code

CLABSI: central line-associated bloodstream infection

CMRP: Certified Materials & Resource Professional

CMS: Centers for Medicare & Medicaid Services

CQO: cost, quality, and outcomes

DRG: diagnosis-related group

EDI: electronic data interchange

EHR: electronic health record

ERP: enterprise resource planning system

GLN: Global Location Number

GPO: group purchasing organization

GTIN: Global Trade Item Number

HCPCS: Health Care Procedure Coding System number

HIPAA: Health Insurance Portability and Accountability Act

HRO: high reliability organization

IHI: Institute for Healthcare Improvement

JIT: just-in-time

LUM: low or logical unit of measure

MMIS: materials management information system

OR: operating room

PAPR: powered air purifying respirator

PAR: periodic automatic replenishment

PO: purchase order

RFID: radio frequency identification

ROI: return on investment

SDP: single-donor platelets

UDI: unique device identification

UNSPSC: United Nations Standard Products and Services Code

UOM: unit of measure

VMI: vendor-managed inventory